The Catholic Field Guide to the Liturgy

Michele E. Chronister
© 2018
All Rights Reserved

©2018
All rights reserved.

Genre: [Catholic Liturgy] [Catechesis]
Summary: a pictorial guide to various items, vestments and vessels used in the Roman Catholic Mass

ISBN-13: 978-1547152216
ISBN-10: 1547152214

Another My Domestic Monastery publication. For more info, visit:
http://www.mydomesticmonastery.com

This book is dedicated to my husband, Andrew, who shares my love for the Mass, for my children (Therese, Maria, Gabriel, and Zelie), my godchildren (Rosie, Arabella, Johnny, Louis, Michael, Max, Nina, Hero, and Rico), Dr. David Fagerberg (who gave me a love for the Theology of the Mass), and to the wonderful priests and seminarians at Kenrick-Glennon Seminary — I loved the Mass and the Sacraments from the time I was a child, but your dedication to the Liturgy makes me love it more than ever before. Thank you for giving God your "yes." Special thanks to Deacon (soon to be Father) Taylor Leffler, who befriended our family, and has answered countless texted questions.

Special thanks to my fellow liturgy loving friends on Facebook, too, for their advice and wisdom.

Introduction

From the time that I was a very small child, I loved the Mass. When I was old enough to become an altar server, and then later a lector, extraordinary minister of Holy Communion, and sacristan, I fell in love with the sacristy.

I loved learning the names of the sacred vessels, loved seeing the closetful of the priest's chasubles, and I loved learning more about the symbolism and meaning behind each of the things that I saw at Mass. Now as a mother, I see my children have the same interest and inquisitiveness.

As one of the sacristans at our parish, I love seeing my children playing, praying, and helping around our church. I love that they feel comfortable chatting with our priests in the sacristy after Mass (even bringing a new teddy bear back to the sacristy because, "Father hasn't seen my new bear before!"), and that they enjoy helping change the altar cloths.

I love seeing them so at home in our church. That is what we are all called to experience. We are called to recognize the church as our home, a foretaste of our *heavenly* home.

There is a comfort in knowing the names of things, in understanding the rich symbolism of our Catholic faith. Being able to name things helps us to feel more at home.

This book is a guide for anyone—children and adults alike—who would like to learn more about the beautiful things that are present at every Mass. With hand-painted watercolor illustrations, and theologically rich descriptions, I hope and pray that this book will be a treasure in your home. It is a Catholic "field guide"—a guide to help you and your family and friends learn the names of what they see and learn more about this rich faith we profess.

—Michele E. Chronister

Church Map

Sacristy

Sanctuary

Nave

Vestibule/Narthex

Contents

The contents of this field guide have been divided into the following categories, based on their purpose. There is also an alphabetical index included at the end of this book.

Vestments............................9

Devotional Prayer....................35

Parts of a Church......................53

Vessels, Cloths, and Objects........75

Books...................................143

Vestments

During the Mass, special garments are worn by the ordained. The following section is a guide to the various garments worn by seminarians, deacons, priests, bishops, cardinals, and the pope.

Alb

Location: worn by priest or deacon, stored in sacristy
Used during Mass: yes
Description:
A long white garment worn by the priest or deacon. It is worn underneath his stole and other vestments (such as the chasuble or dalmatic), and over the amice and cassock. It is tied around the waist with a cincture. This garment is like tunics worn by the ancient Greeks and Romans, and it is meant to call to mind the white garments worn at Baptism. Because it is white, it is also meant to remind the priest that he is called to purity—total devotion and love for God and the Church.

11

Amice

Location: worn by a priest or deacon, stored in sacristy
Used during Mass: yes
Description:
A simple white cloth that the priest or deacon wears around his neck, it protects the alb and chasuble (and dalmatic, in the case of the deacon) from becoming dirty or stained. Amices can be frequently washed and changed, while albs and chasubles are cleaned less frequently.

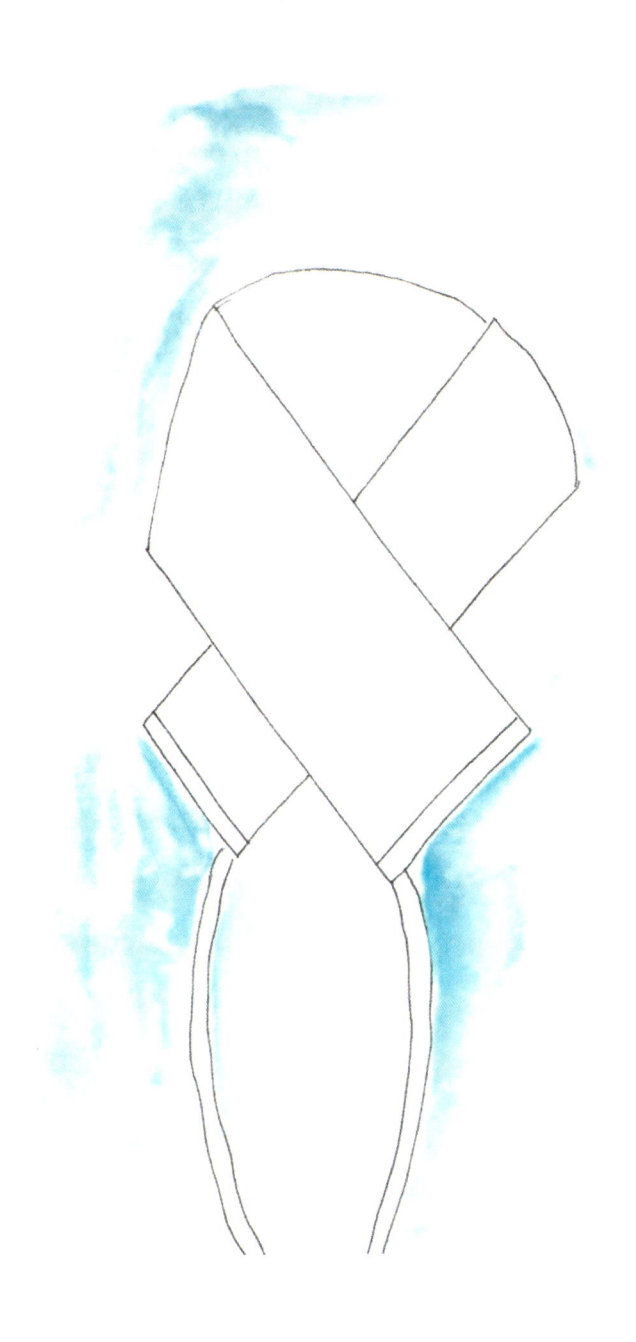

Biretta

Location: worn by a priest
Used during Mass: sometimes
Description:
A hat that may be worn by Catholic clergy. When worn by a priest, the biretta is black, a bishop's is pink, and a cardinal's is red. (A monsignor wears a black biretta with a purple tuft.)

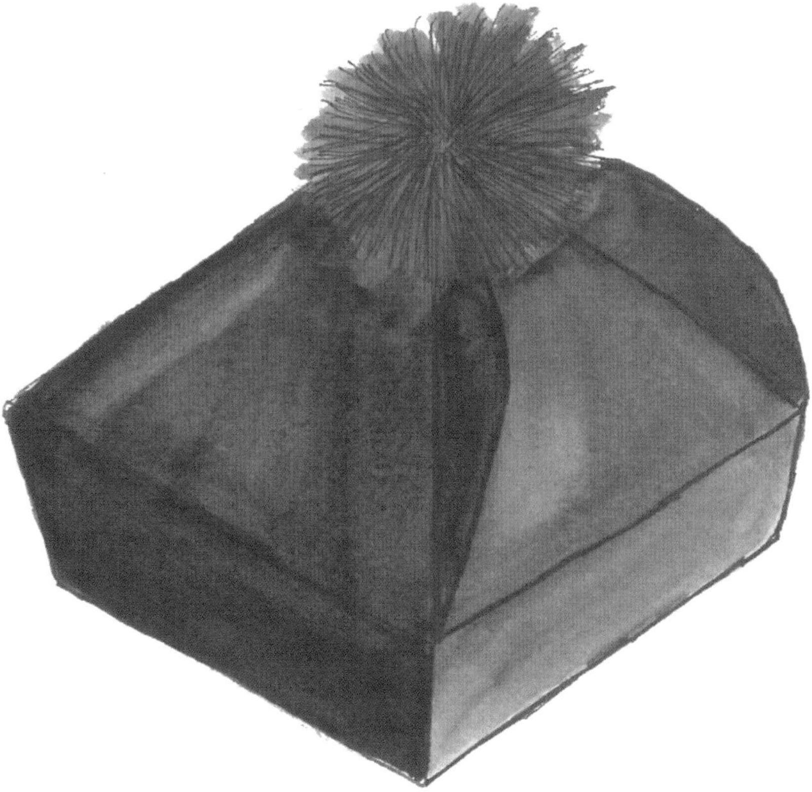

Cassock

Location: worn by seminarian or priest
Used during Mass: sometimes
Description:
This long, black garment is worn by a priest as part of his clerical garb. It may also be worn by a monsignor, with a purple belt and buttons. A bishop may wear a black one (with pink belt and buttons) or a pink cassock. A cardinal may do the same with the color red. The pope wears a white cassock. When a surplice is worn, a cassock is always worn beneath. A cassock may be worn outside of Mass.

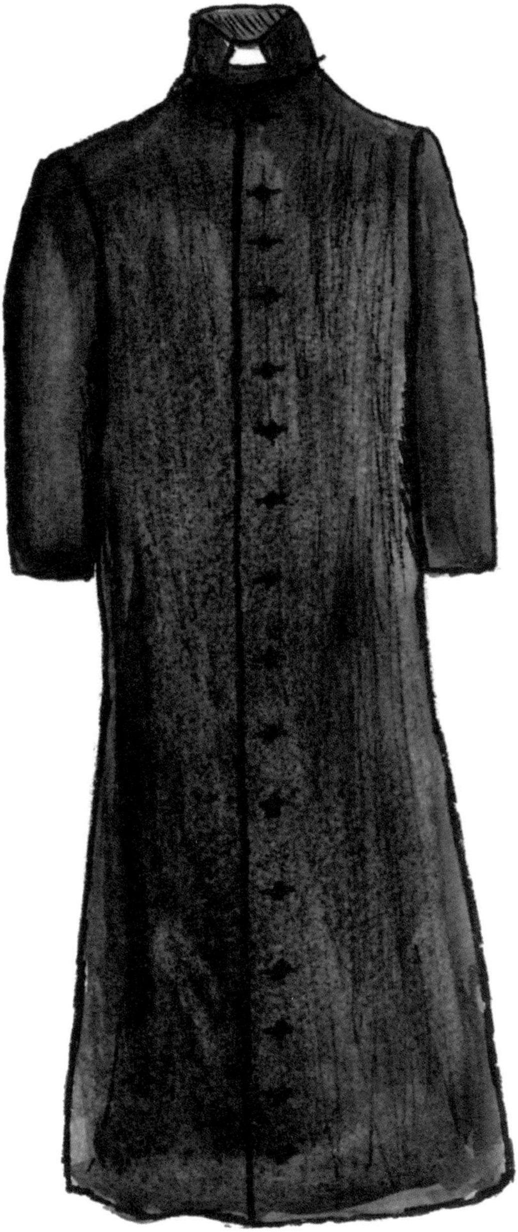

Chasuble

Location: worn by priest, stored in sacristy
Used during Mass: yes
Description:
The chasuble is the outermost of the vestments worn by the priest at Mass. Chasubles come in a variety of different colors, based on the liturgical season. Purple is worn for Lent and Advent, green for Ordinary Time, rose for Gaudete and Laetare Sunday, red for Pentecost, Good Friday, Palm Sunday, and feasts of saints who were martyrs (who died for their faith in Jesus), white (or gold) for Easter, Christmas, Holy Thursday, funerals, and for great feasts and solemnities, and black for funerals or All Souls Day/Masses offered for the poor souls in purgatory (typically during the month of November). Chasubles also come in a variety of styles, including the gothic (top row), roman, and "fiddleback" (bottom row, similar to roman).

19

Cincture

Location: worn by priest or deacon, stored in sacristy
Used during Mass: yes
Description:
A simple cord worn with an alb and tied at the waist, it is often white, but may vary with clerical position (i.e., priest vs. bishop).

21

Cope

Location: worn by priest or deacon, stored in sacristy
Used during Mass: no
Description:
This cape-like vestment may be worn as the outer vestment by the priest, in sacramental celebrations outside of the Mass. It is also used for liturgical gatherings outside of the Mass, such as Eucharist adoration and processions, and in that instance may be worn with a humeral veil on top of the cope (a sign of reverence for Jesus in Eucharist).

23

Dalmatic

Location: worn by deacon, stored in sacristy
Used during Mass: yes
Description:
This vestment may be worn by the deacon at Mass, over the alb, cincture, amice, and stole. (A deacon may also choose to wear just a stole over his alb.) It is designed to match the chasuble of the priest, and its color is determined by the liturgical season or feastday.

25

Miter

Location: worn by an abbot or bishop, stored in cathedral sacristy
Used during Mass: yes
Description:
This tall hat is worn by an abbot, bishop, archbishop, cardinal, or pope as part of his vestments during the Mass. It is removed during prayer (such as during the Eucharistic prayer, when even the zucchetto is removed) as a sign of reverence for God.

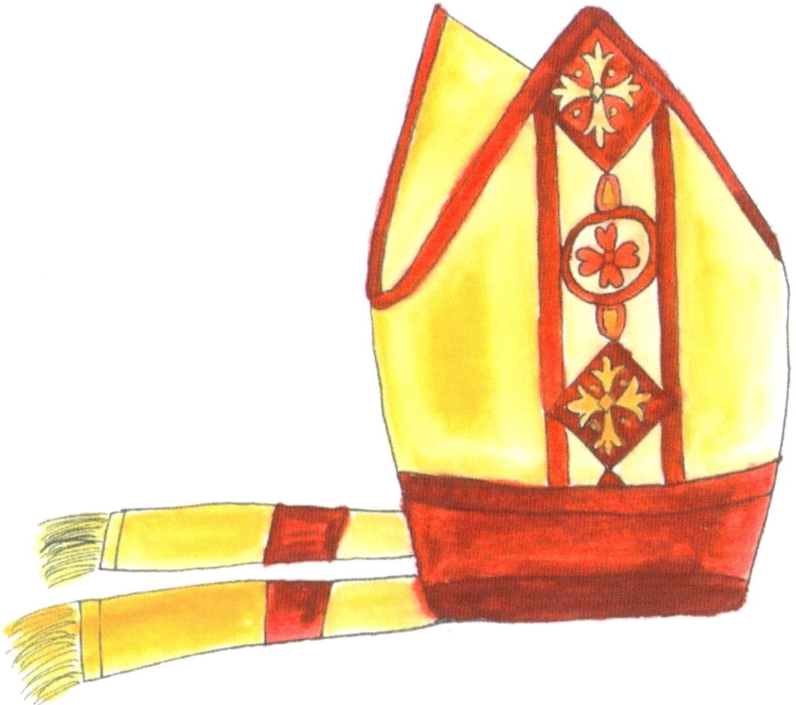

Stole

Location: worn by priest or deacon, stored in sacristy
Used during Mass: yes
Description:
Worn by a priest or deacon (or bishop, cardinal or pope) when he is performing the duties of the ordained (such as saying or assisting at Mass, hearing Confessions, baptizing a person, etc.), as part of his vestments. The stole is worn over the alb, but underneath a chasuble or dalmatic (when worn at Mass). A priest may celebrate Mass or the sacraments in just an alb and stole. The deacon's stole is worn from his shoulder to his hips (as on the right) and the priest's is draped around his neck (as on the left). It is a sign of the ordained priest taking up the cross or "yoke" of Christ. The deacon or priest kisses the stole before putting it on.

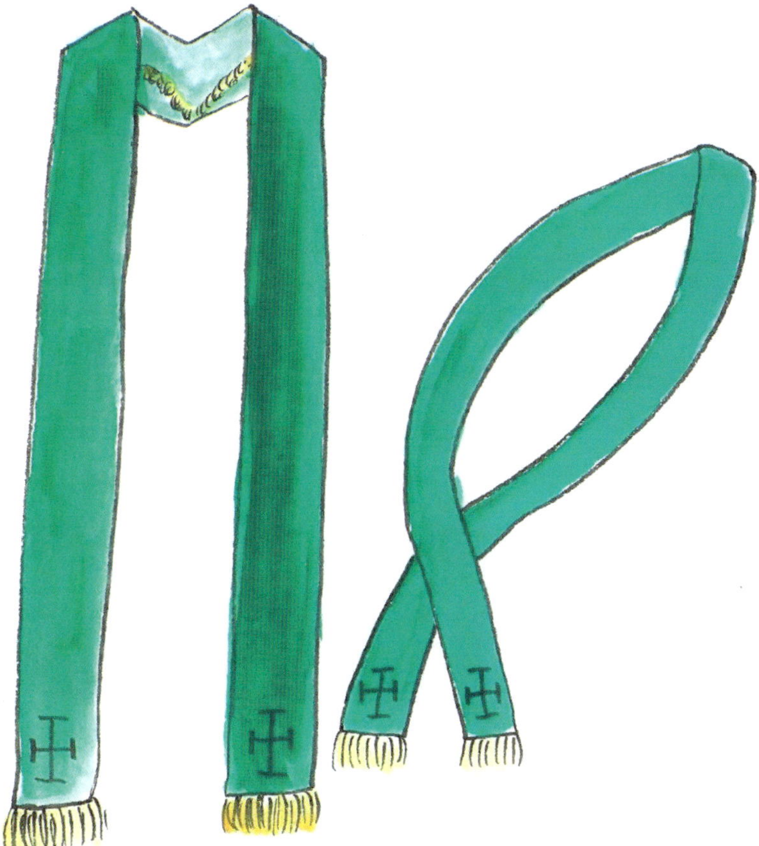

Surplice

Location: worn by priest, deacon, or seminarian
Used during Mass: sometimes
Description:
The surplice is another part of the garments that may be worn by a seminarian, deacon, priest, bishop, cardinal, or pope. This white garment is worn over a cassock, and in the case of the ordained, the stole is worn on top of the surplice. The surplice often has liturgically appropriate lace (i.e. adorned with religious imagery).

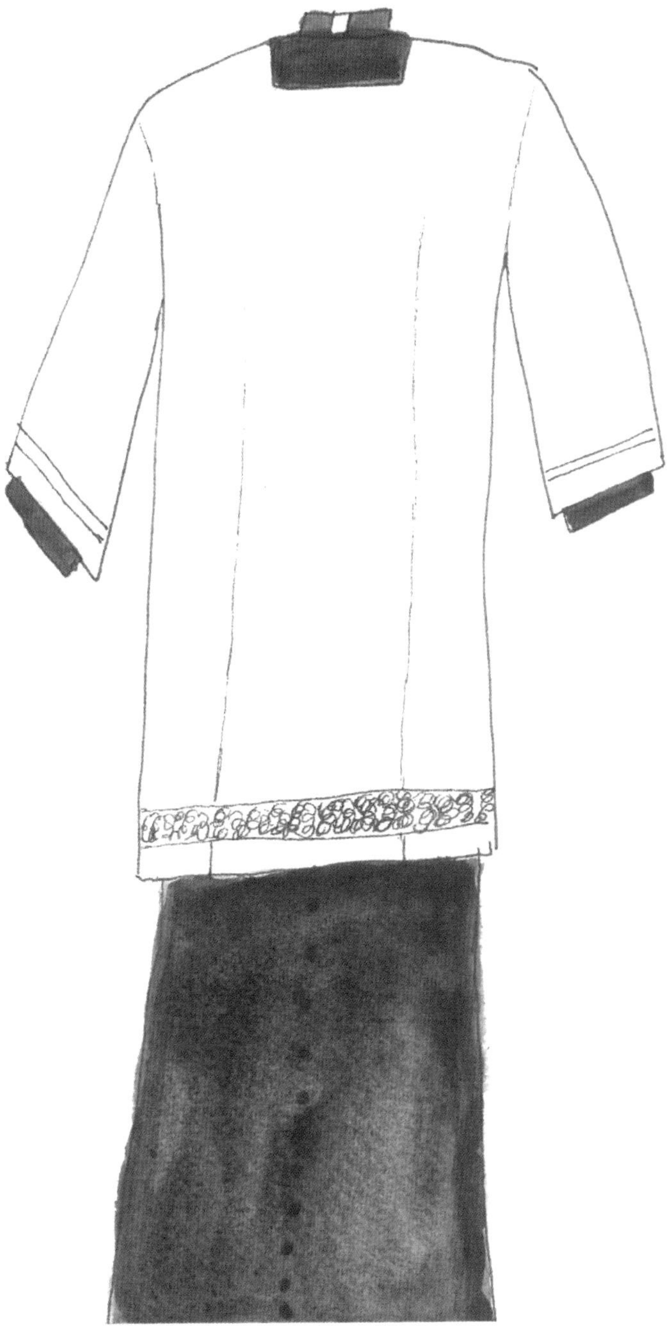

Zucchetto

Location: most commonly worn by a bishop
Used during Mass: yes (also worn outside of Mass)
Description:
A simple hat worn as part of the garments of the priest (historically, although not as commonly seen as it once was), monsignor, bishop, cardinal, or pope. It is most commonly worn by a bishop. The color is determined by the role that that person plays in the church (i.e. purple for monsignor, pink for bishop, red for cardinal, and white for the pope). It is always removed during the Eucharistic prayer at Mass, as a sign of humility and reverence before Christ in the Eucharist.

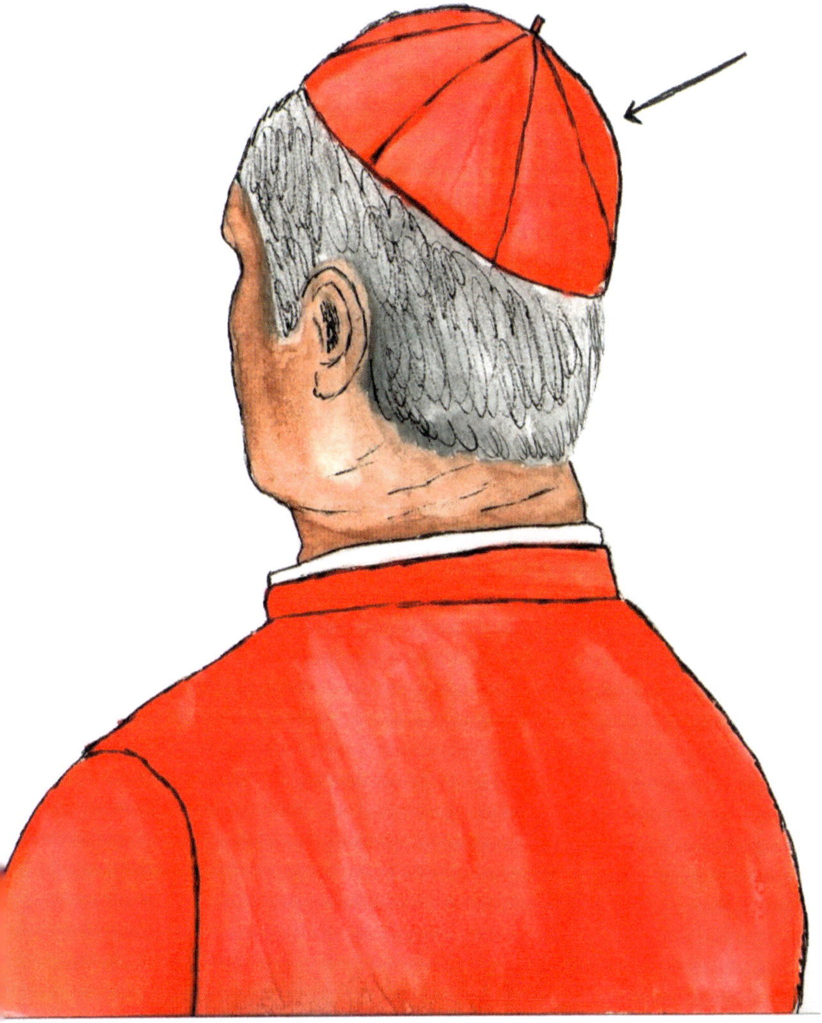

Devotional Prayer

The following objects are used to assist the faithful in devotional prayer. Devotional prayer may include personal prayer, as well as communal prayer outside of Mass.

Holy Water Font

Location: at the entrances to the nave

Used during Mass: no (used prior to and after Mass)

Description:

Found at the entrances of the church, this font always contains holy water (except during the Triduum, when it is emptied). As the faithful enter the church and bless themselves, they call to mind their own Baptism. Devoutly blessing oneself with holy water also removes all venial sin from a person's soul.

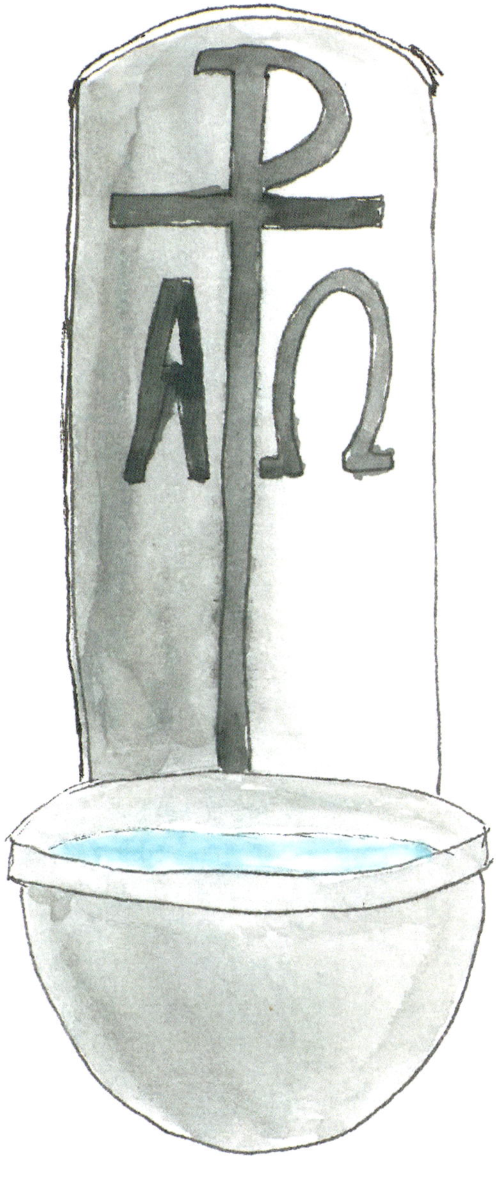

Icon

Location: nave or sanctuary
Used during Mass: yes (may be used for personal prayer)
Description:
An icon is a beautiful image of Jesus, Mary, another saint, or an episode from Scripture. Icons are said to be "written" as they tell of the Word of God and are often completed over a long period of time. The writing of icons involves much prayer on the part of the "writer," and is typically done in a particularly recognizable style (Byzantine, Russian, etc.). These beautiful images can be found in the church and are meant to be a tool to assist the faithful in their prayer and meditation on the Scriptures and truths of the faith. Icons may also be hung in homes of the faithful.

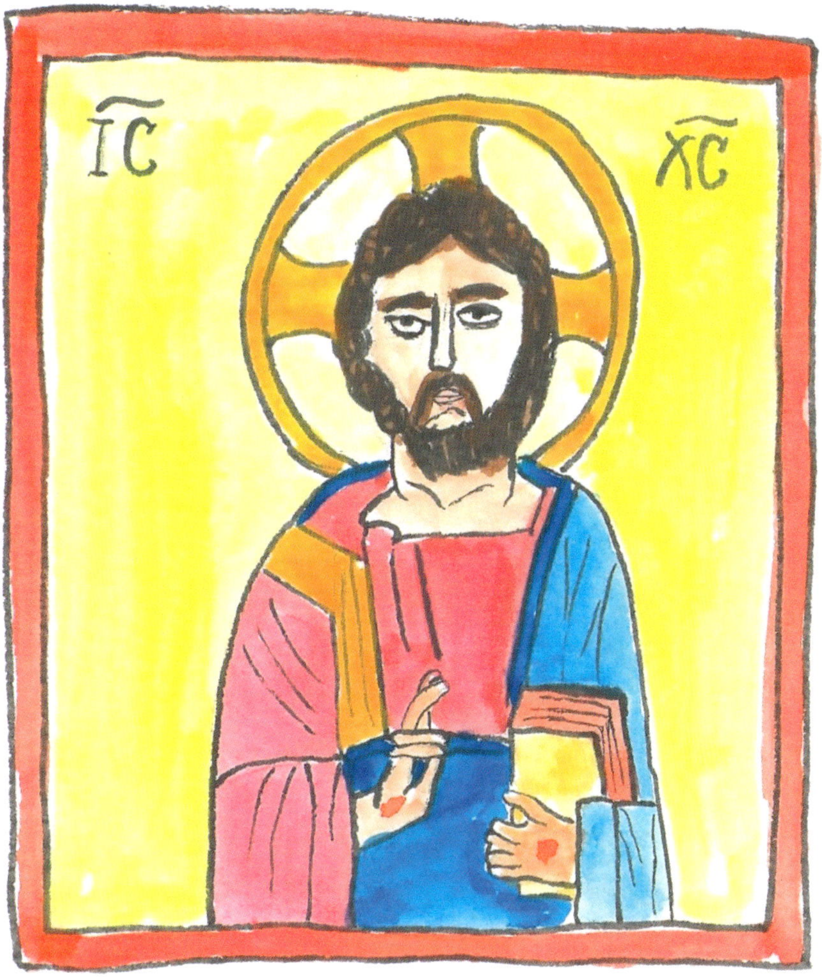
IC
XC

Kneeler

Location: nave and sanctuary
Used during Mass: yes
Description:
Found in the church, kneelers assist the faithful in showing reverence during Mass or personal prayer. Kneelers are often built into pews, and individual ones may be found in the sanctuary or by smaller shrines in the church. As Catholics, we kneel when we pray, as a reminder of our littleness in the presence of God. When we kneel before a statue or holy image, we are not worshipping it. Rather, the statue or image helps us to raise our thoughts to God, and our kneeling is directed toward praise and worship of God alone.

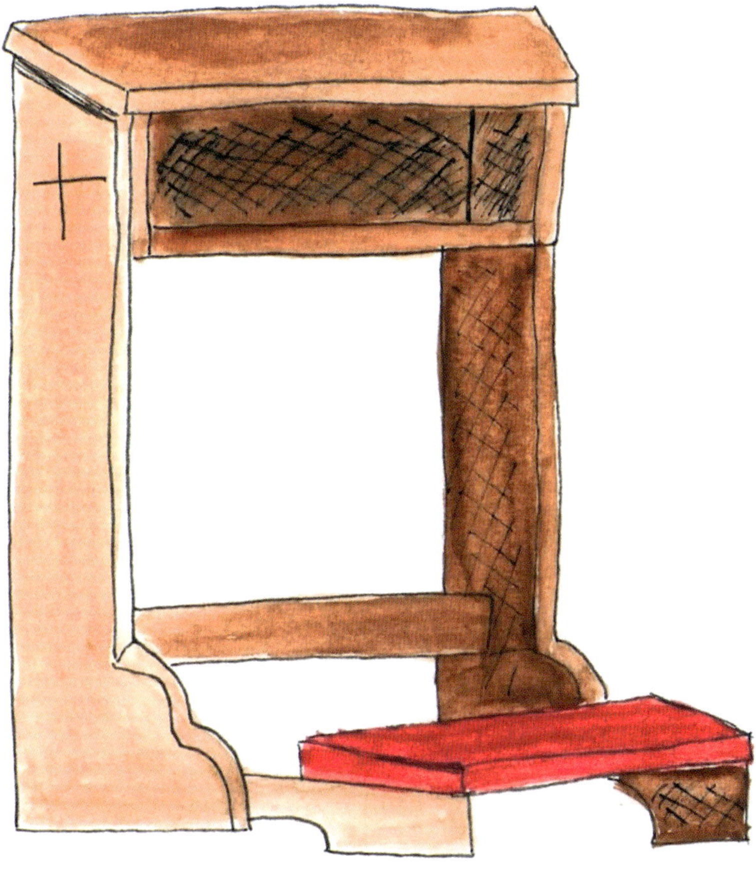

Monstrance

Location: on the altar during adoration, stored in the sacristy
Used during Mass: no
Description:
This beautiful vessel (often modeled on a sunburst) contains the Body of Christ for use during Exposition (adoration where Jesus is visible in a monstrance instead of in the tabernacle) or Eucharistic processions. Through the center glass window, the Body of Christ can be seen and adored. As a sign of reverence for Christ, who is king, it is made of gold or silver, and may be decorated with precious gems.

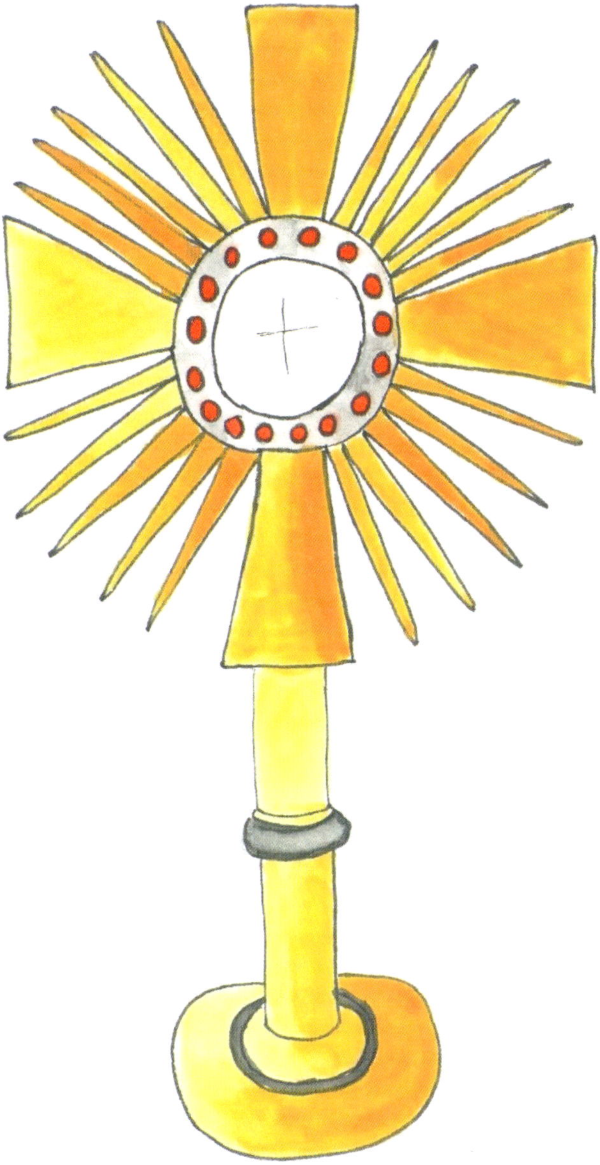

Processional Canopy

Location: used in outdoor eucharistic processions
Used during Mass: no
Description:
This beautiful canopy (typically made of beautiful silken, embroidered material) is used in Eucharistic processions. It is carried over the priest who elevates Jesus in the monstrance for all to see. It is another way of showing reverence for the Eucharist.

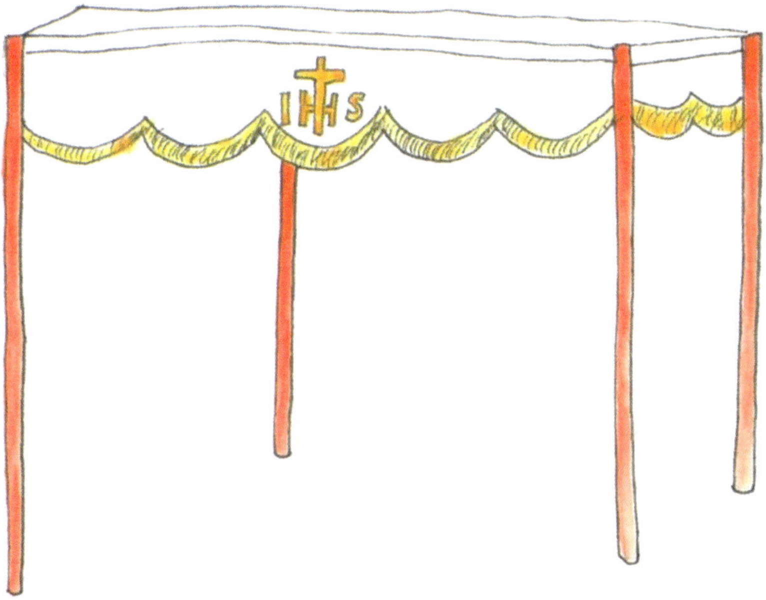
IHS

Reliquary

Location: at a side altar or shrine
Used during Mass: no
Description:
This golden case is used to hold and display relics. Relics are matter associated with the saints. A first class relic is one that is a piece of the saint's body (such as bone, hair, etc.), a second class relic is one that touched the saint's body (such as a piece of clothing), and a third class relic is one that has touched a first or second class relic (can be fabric, a rosary or sacramental, etc.). The point of relics is not to show worship to the saints (since worship is for God alone) but to allow us a closer connection to the saints (like the way families cling to physical reminders of loved ones who have died). Relics are venerated – treated with special care. One way to venerate relics is to kiss them, the way one would kiss a picture of a loved one.

Stations of the Cross
Location: nave
Used during Mass: no
Description:
These images of Christ's Way of the Cross are hung on the walls of the church, serving as aides in personal and public prayer. They are a way for the faithful to pray this prayer when they are unable to walk the original Way of the Cross in Jerusalem. They call to mind the suffering of Jesus as he carried his cross to Calvary

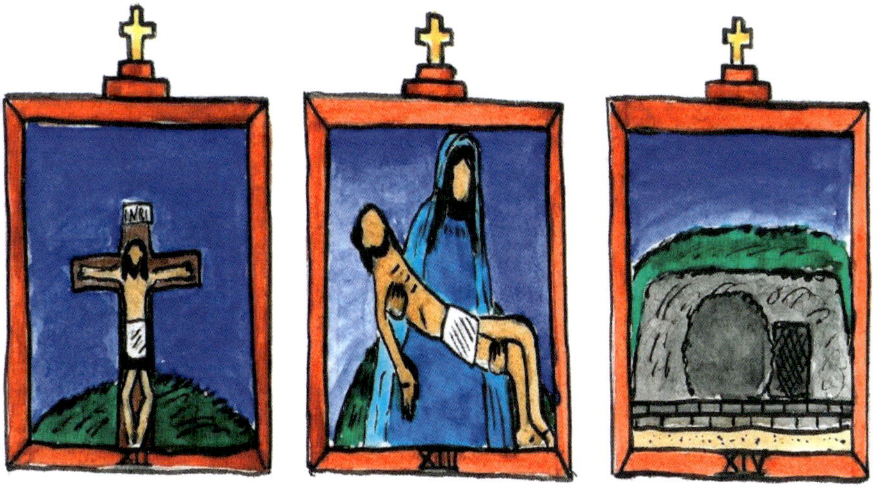

Votive Candles

Location: side altar or shrine
Used during Mass: no (although they may remain lit during Mass)
Description:
Typically found at a side altar or shrine in the church, votive candles are lit by the faithful. Each lit candle is a reminder of a prayer intention of a member of the faithful, meant to symbolize the prayer being brought to God and heard by him, even long after the person who lit it has left the church building. Votive candles are sometimes found by a picture, icon, or statue of a saint, as a symbol of asking our brothers and sisters in heaven to join us in praying to God for our intentions.

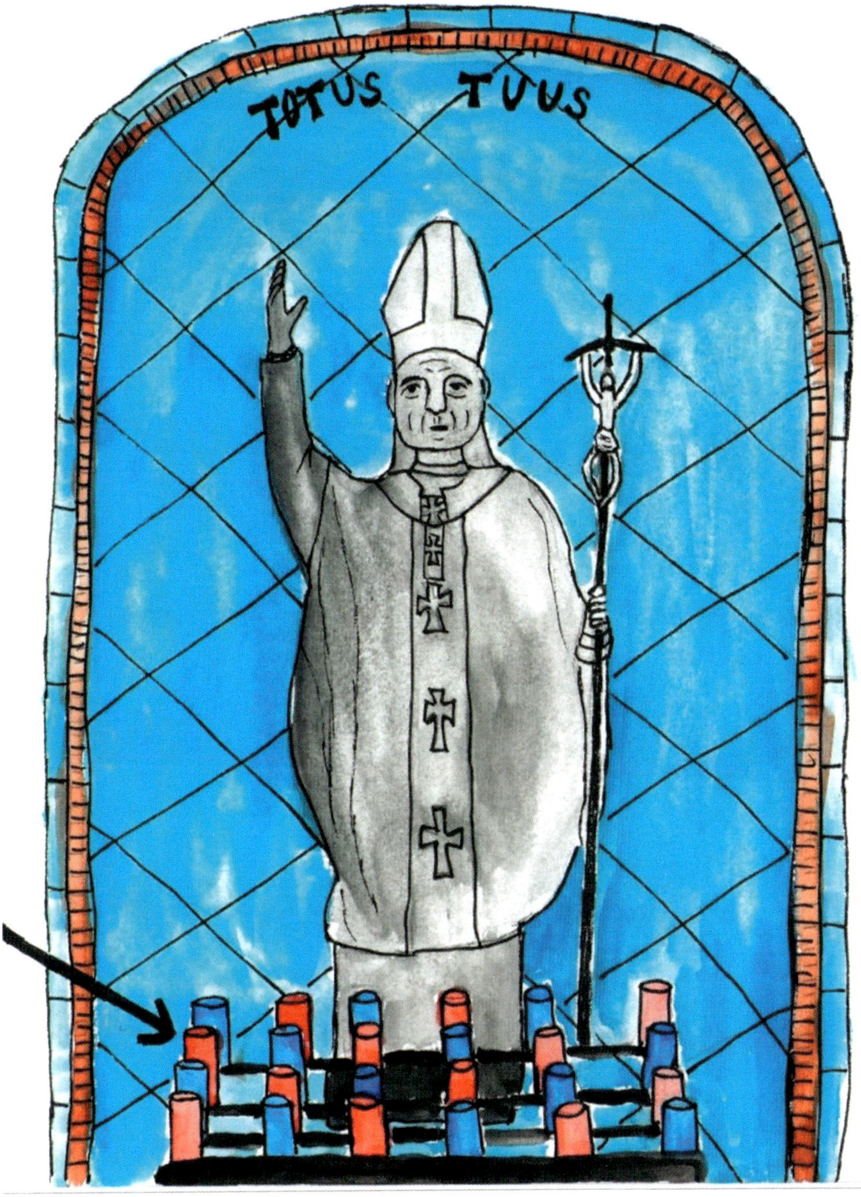
TOTUS TUUS

Parts of a Church

Every Catholic church looks a little bit different, but there are some things found in *all* Catholic churches, and other things that are found in *many* churches. Following are things you will find in a Catholic church.

Altar

Location: sanctuary
Used during Mass: yes
Description:
Because the Eucharist is both a meal and a sacrifice, the altar is a table *and* also represents Christ and his perfect sacrifice. The sacrifice of the Mass is offered on the altar, where Christ's sacrifice is re-presented. Unlike in the time before Christ, a new sacrifice is not offered at each Mass, but rather Christ's one, perfect sacrifice is made present again. Because the altar represents Christ we bow to the altar, in order to show reverence. The altar must contain some stone or be made entirely of stone, and it also contains a relic of a saint. Other than on Good Friday, it should always be covered with an altar cloth.

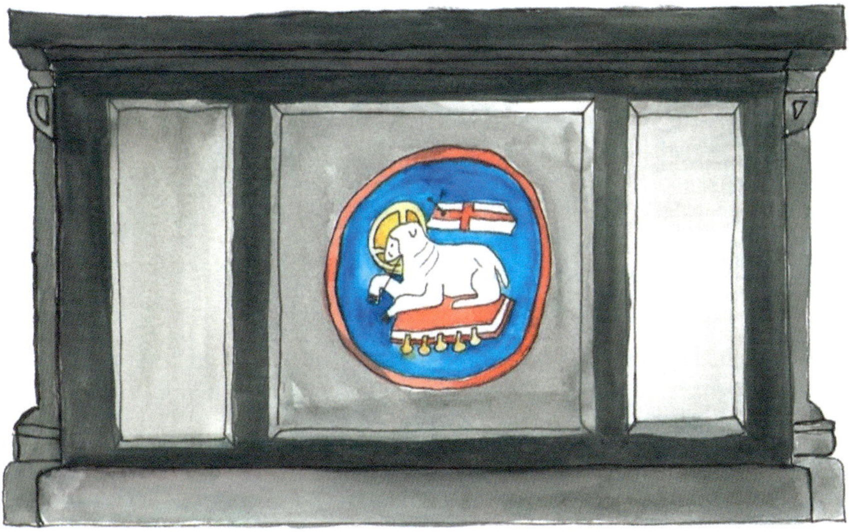

Ambo

Location: sanctuary
Used during Mass: yes
Description:
Readings from the Bible (also known as the Scripture readings) are proclaimed from here during the Liturgy of the Word. The Lector proclaims the First Reading, the Lector or a Cantor leads the Responsorial Psalm, and the Lector then reads the Second Reading (which is only present on Sundays and special holy feasts, such as Solemnities). Following the Alleluia, the deacon or priest proclaims the Gospel from the ambo, and then preaches the homily.

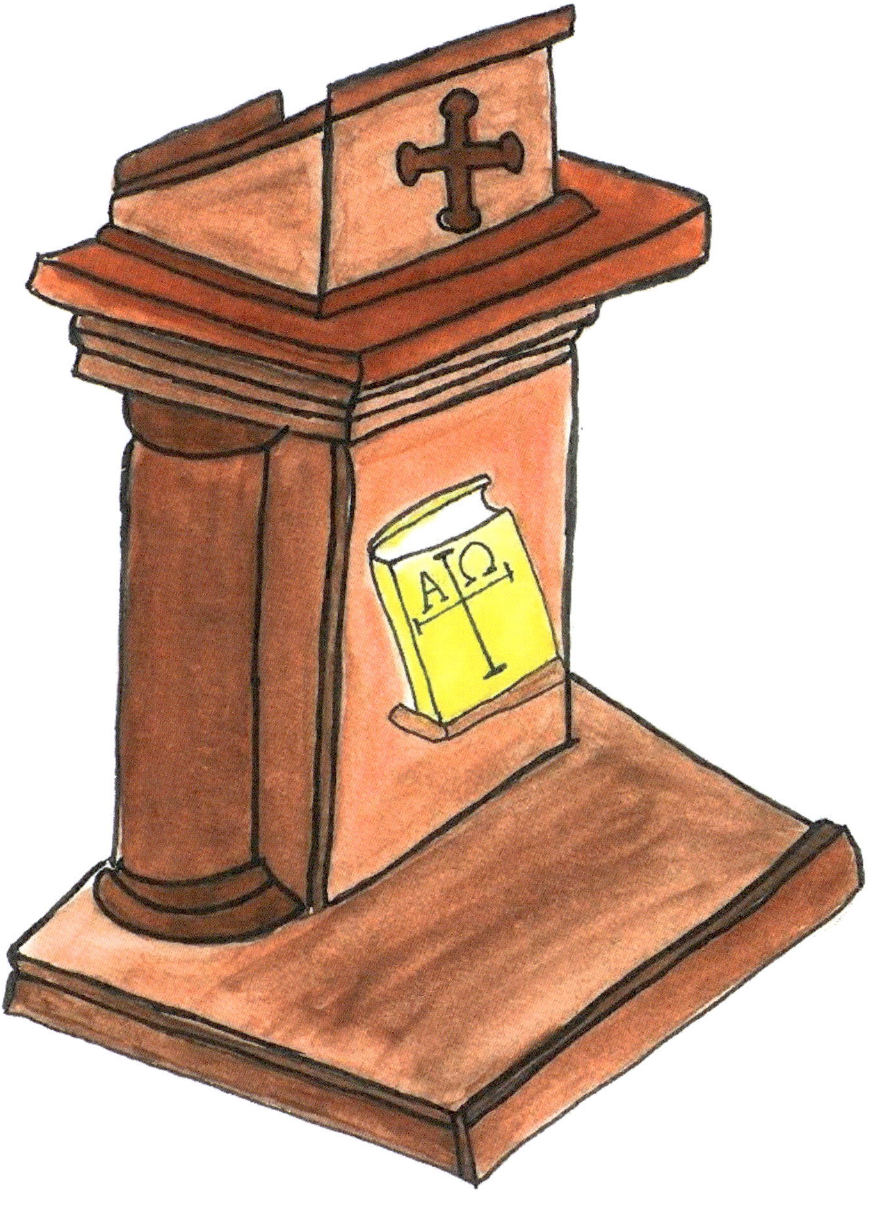
A
Ω

Baldacchino

Location: sanctuary
Used during Mass: yes
Description:
This canopy over the altar is usually made of wood or stone. The most famous example is in St. Peter's Basilica in Rome. The canopy bears witness to the greatness and importance of the altar. It also calls to mind the tent used by the people of Israel in the Old Testament to cover the Ark of the Covenant.

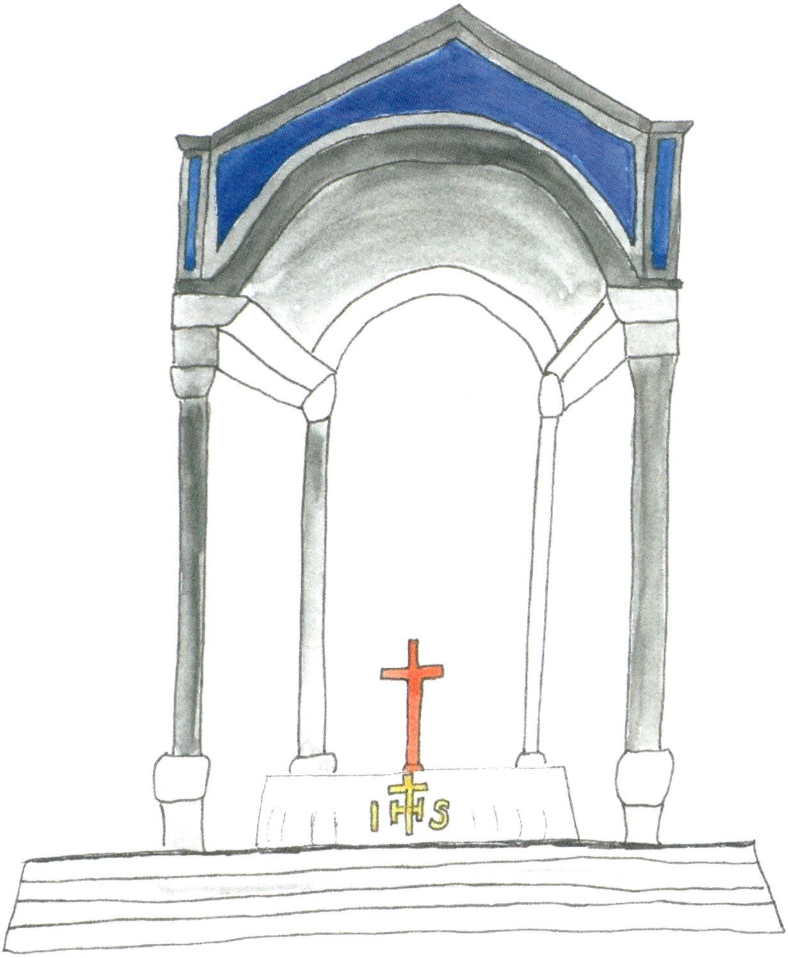
IHS

Baptismal Font

Location: sanctuary, nave, or baptistry
Used during Mass: sometimes
Description:
This is where Baptisms take place. It is where holy water is poured over the head of each new Christian (or, in some cases, where the new Christian is fully immersed in the water), while the words of Baptism are prayed, "[Name], I baptize you in the name of the Father, and of the Son, and of the Holy Spirit." It is also called the "womb of the Church." Just as a baby grows and is born from his or her mother's womb, new Catholics are born out of this font.

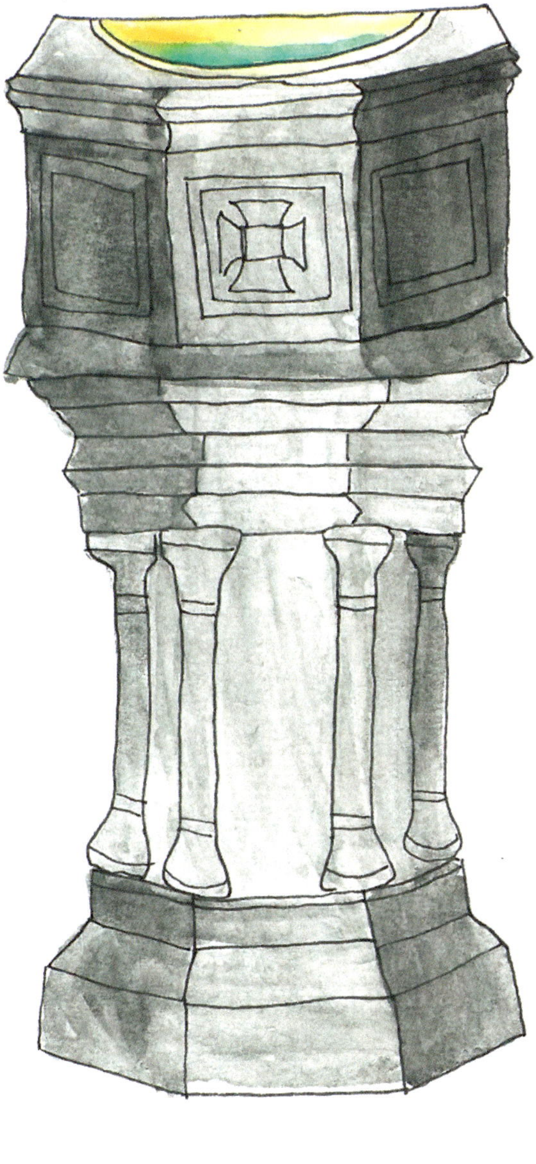

Confessional
Location: nave
Used during Mass: no
Description:
The Sacrament of Reconciliation (also known as "Confession") is typically celebrated here (although it may be celebrated outside of the Confessional, as well). The priest sits on one side of the confessional, and the penitent kneels behind a screen or sits in a chair (face-to-face with the priest) on the other side of the confessional. It is a place of great joy and renewal for the Church. Although the penitent (the person going to Confession) enters in sorrow, he or she leaves rejoicing...and all the Church rejoices, too. The keys at the top of this confessional remind us of Jesus' words to Peter—that whatever Peter and his successors bind or loose on earth will be so in heaven. After the resurrection, Jesus also tells the Apostles that whatever sins they forgive will be forgiven. Through these promises, Jesus gave the Church the gift of this sacrament. In Confession, the priest absolves sins *in persona Christi* – "in the person of Christ." Christ is the one who forgives sins, working through the person of the priest.

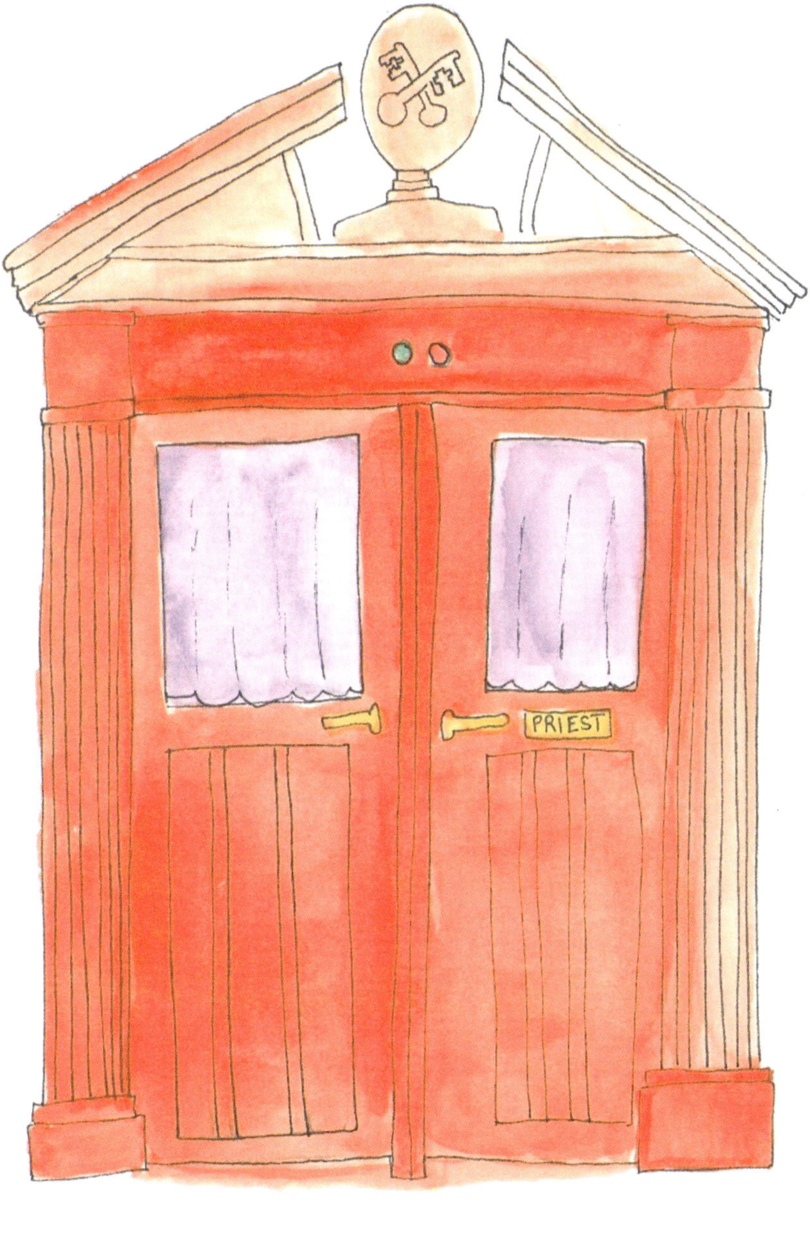
PRIEST

Nave

Location: main body of church building
Used during Mass: yes
Description:
The nave is the central part of the church, where the faithful assemble for the liturgy. A church is sometimes called the "barque" or boat, of St. Peter. Peter was originally a fisherman, until Jesus called him to be a "fisher of men." This is the call of all priests. The nave is meant to resemble a boat, carrying those who are journeying to heaven.

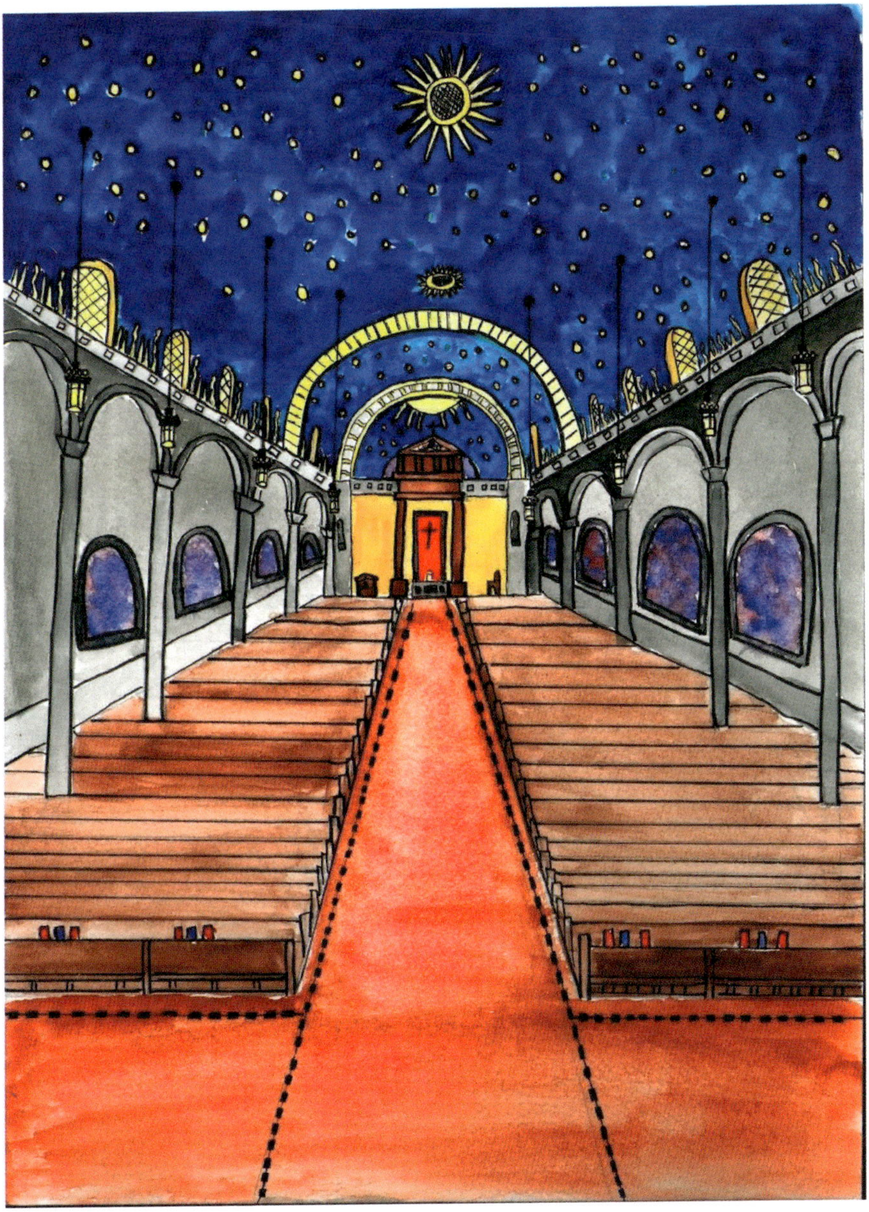

Sacrarium

Location: sacristy
Used during Mass: no
Description:

This special sink empties directly into the ground, rather than into the sewer. It is for disposing of holy water, or water used in purifying vessels or cloths that have come in contact with the Eucharist. Leftover Precious Blood should be consumed by the priest or extraordinary minister, not poured down the sacrarium. This sink allows any particles of the Eucharist to be disposed of with reverence and dignity.

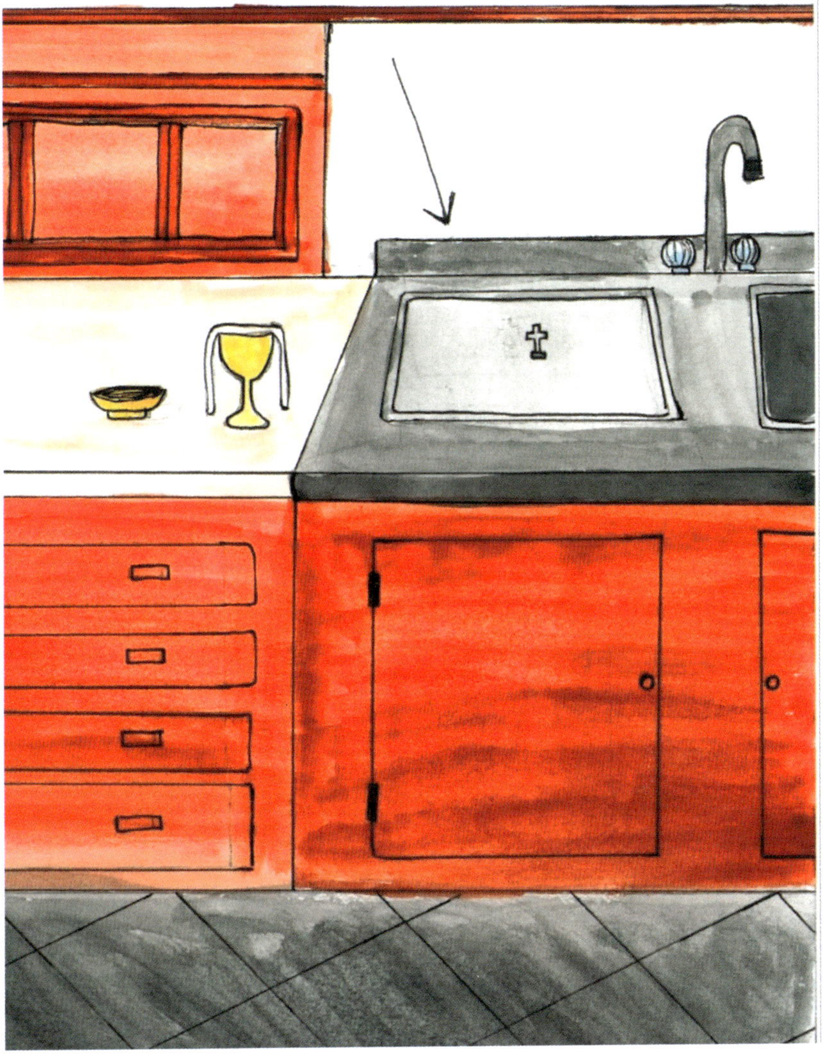

Sacristy

Location: typically, behind or to side of the sanctuary, sometimes adjoining the vestibule

Used during Mass: no

Description:

The sacristy is the room where all the vessels, altar cloths, and vestments are stored when not in use. It is also where the priest or sacristan prepares the vessels that will be used during the Mass - filling cruets with water and wine and filling the ciborium with hosts. Sometimes there is a separate sacristy where the priest may put his vestments on (called the "vesting sacristy") but there is often just one sacristy. It should be a place that allows for quiet and prayer for the priest, as he prepares for Mass.

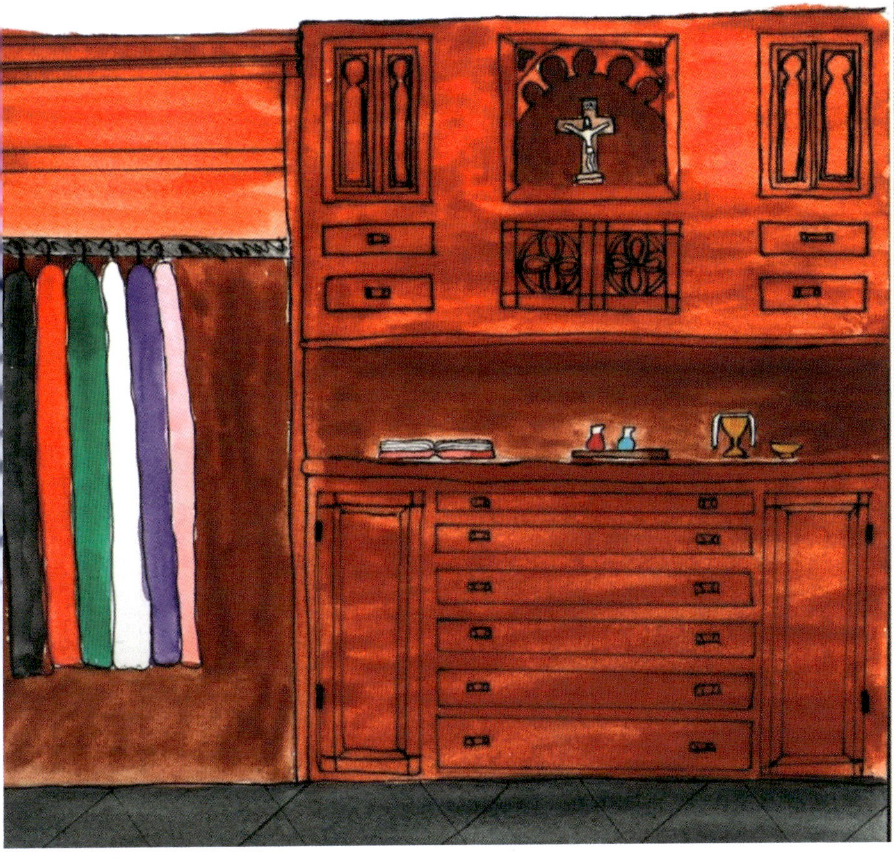

Sanctuary

Location: front of the church interior
Used during Mass: yes
Description:
Although the whole church is a sacred place, the most sacred part of the church is the sanctuary – the place where the altar, tabernacle, presider's chair, and ambo are found. It is typically set apart in some way, such as by stairs and/or an altar rail. This set apartness is a visual reminder of the sacredness of what happens on the altar at each Mass.

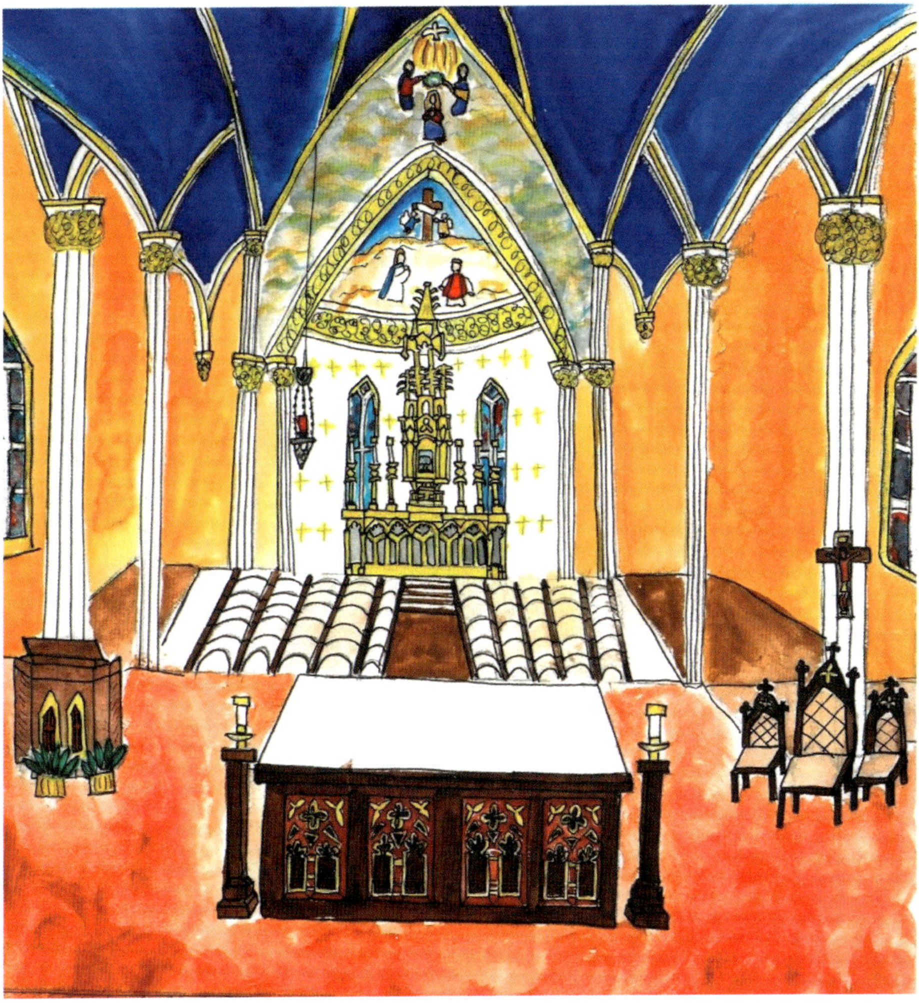

Vestibule

Location: back of the church interior
Used during Mass: no
Description:
Serving as an entryway into the church, it assists the faithful in making the transition from the outside world to the nave and sanctuary (which are a foretaste of heaven on earth).

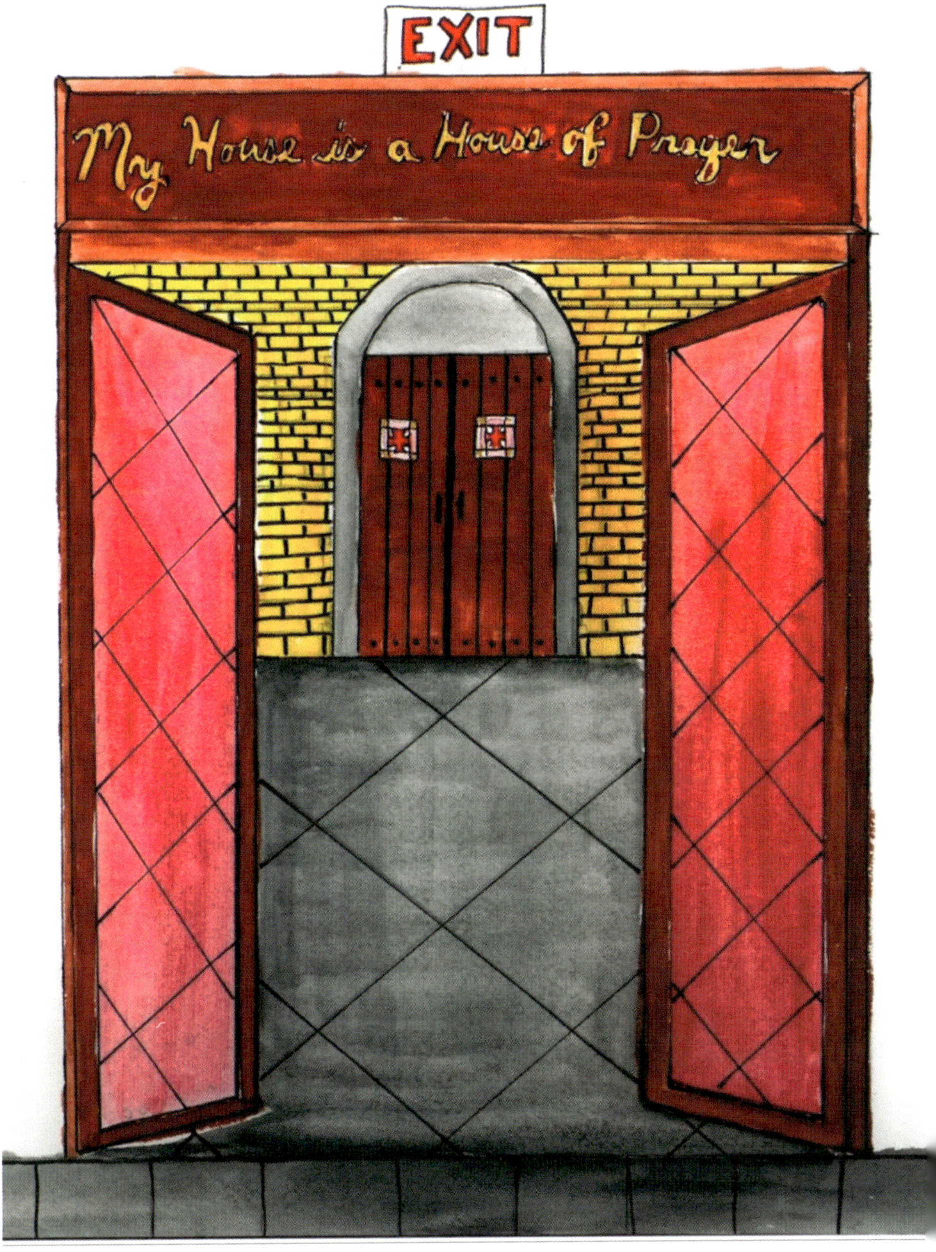
EXIT
My House is a House of Prayer

Vessels, Cloths, and Objects

The Catholic Church offers a feast for the senses – things to taste, touch, hear, smell, and see. The following are various things used to engage the senses, and to offer worship to God that is beautiful and fitting.

Ablution Cup

Location: sanctuary
Used during Mass: yes
Description:
A small cup holding water, it is placed beside the tabernacle. After Communion, the priest or deacon returns the ciborium (the bowl-like container holding Jesus in the Eucharist) to the tabernacle. Afterwards, he dips his fingers in the ablution cup, to rinse them off. This is a way to make sure that none of the tiny particles of the host remain on his fingers and fall to the floor. Since the host is now Jesus, even the smallest particles are truly him, and must be treated with reverence. When this water is changed the old water is poured down the sacrarium, a special sink that empties into the ground instead of the sewer.

Altar Bells

Location: sanctuary
Used during Mass: yes
Description:
These bells are rung by one of the altar servers right after the consecration of the bread and the wine, during the elevation. When the priest elevates (lifts) the bread that has become the Body of Christ, and the chalice of the wine that has become the Blood of Christ, he holds Christ up high for all to love and adore. The bells remind the assembly to look up and pay attention because Christ is now present. When the bells ring, the faithful may pray softly, "My Lord, and my God," or a similar prayer.

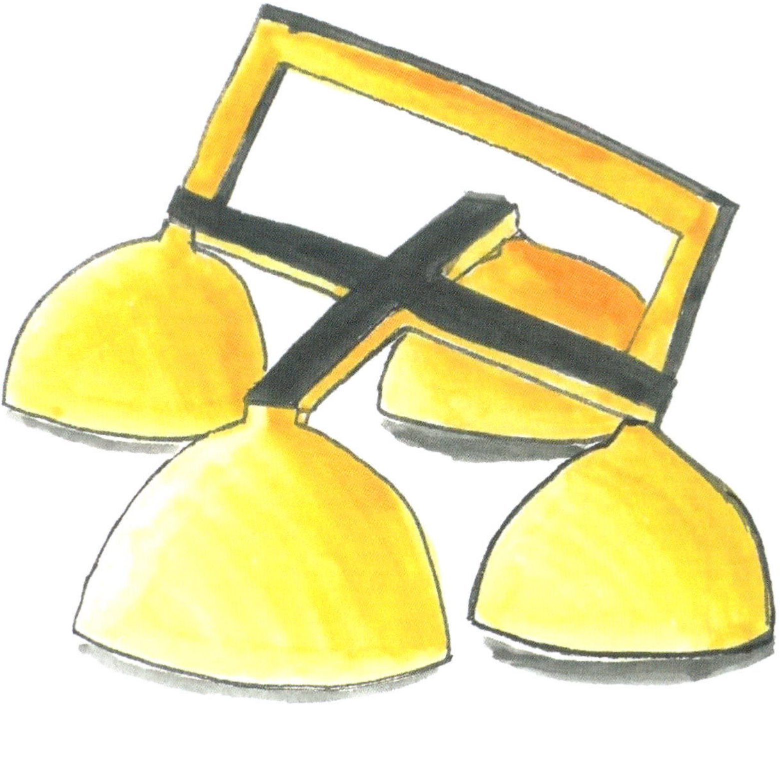

Altar Cloth

Location: sanctuary
Used during Mass: yes
Description:
This beautiful cloth covers the altar during and outside of the Mass. The altar is covered as a sign of reverence, since this is where the bread and wine become the Body and Blood of Christ. In the Ordinary Form of the Mass, a white cloth is required to cover the altar. In the United States, altar cloths of other colors may be used under the white one (e.g., for certain liturgical seasons) but there must always be a white altar cloth on top. In the Extraordinary Form, three altar cloths are layered on top of each other, and a similar layering is sometimes done in the Ordinary Form, as well.

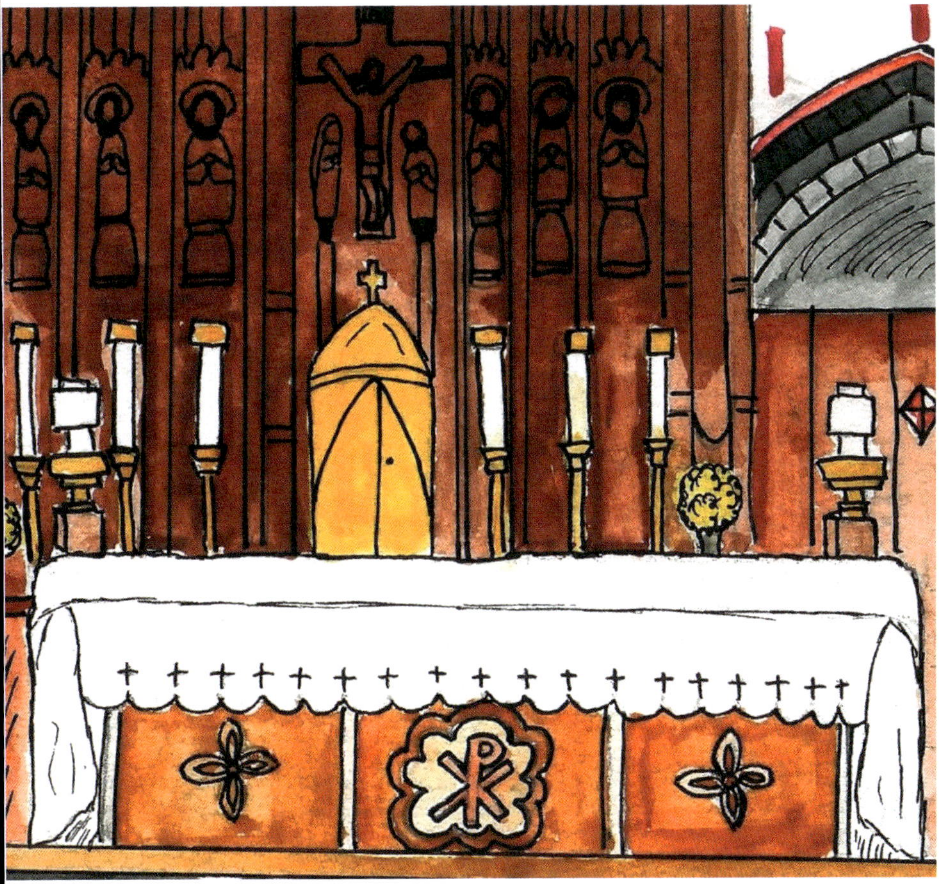

Aspergillum

Location: stored in sacristy
Used during Mass: yes
Description:
Commonly called the "sprinkler," the aspergillum is used to sprinkle holy water on the assembly, or on an item that is being blest. During the Easter season especially, the Rite of Sprinkling may replace the Penitential Rite (where the "Lord Have Mercy" or "Kyrie" is prayed), serving as a reminder of our Baptism and our Baptismal promises, which we renew during this joyous season. (The bucket used to carry the Holy Water is the aspersorium.)

Baptismal Shell

Location: Baptismal font
Used during Mass: sometimes (when Baptisms occur during Mass)
Description:
Typically made of or plated with silver or gold, this beautiful shell is used to pour holy water over the head of the person being baptized. It is not strictly necessary, but it often used because of its rich symbolism. It is a reminder of St. John the Baptist baptizing Jesus in the Jordan River. The shell is also considered an early symbol of the resurrection.

Candle Snuffer

Location: sacristy
Used during Mass: no
Description:
This is used to light candles before Mass and extinguish them afterwards. The wick is pushed up to the top and lit for lighting candles. The bell-shaped snuffer is used to extinguish the candles when Mass has ended.

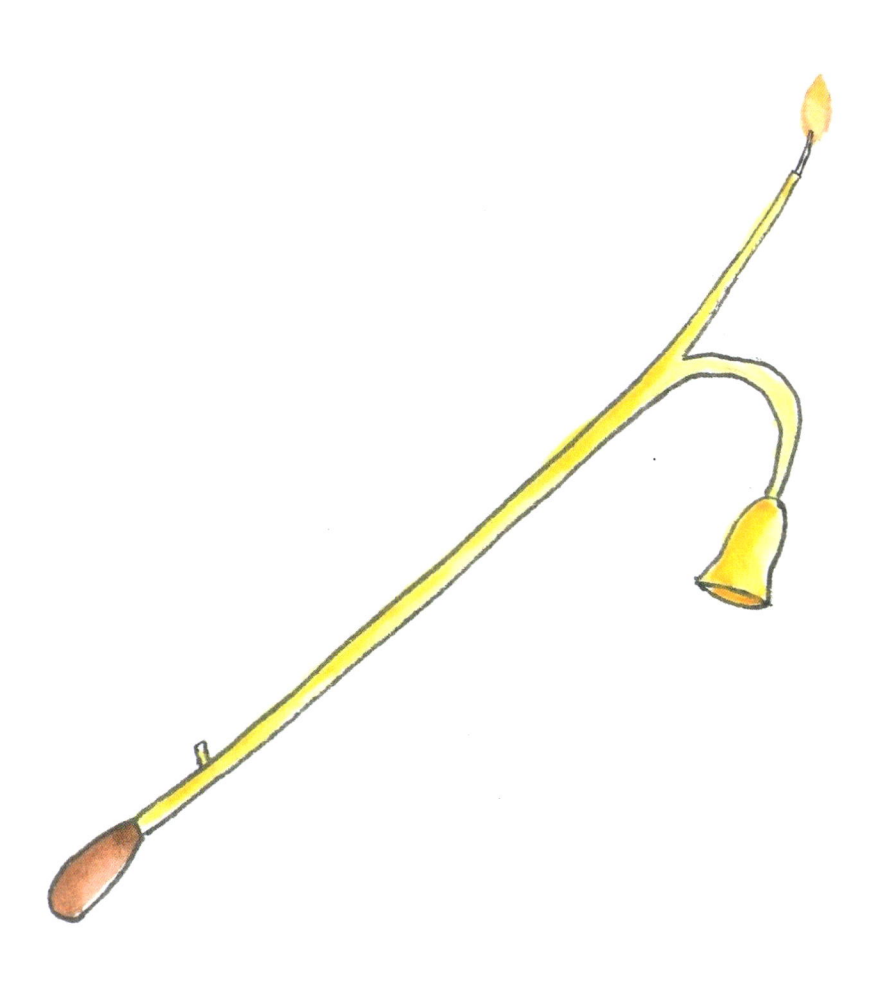

Candles

Location: sanctuary
Used during Mass: yes
Description:
Used at every Mass, candles are a sign of Christ, our Light. They are traditionally made of beeswax, and their aroma is a recognizable scent in any Catholic church. Lighted candles are placed beside or on the altar for the Mass. Candles can also be carried in during the opening procession and recessional and will sometimes be carried to the ambo as part of the procession before the Gospel.

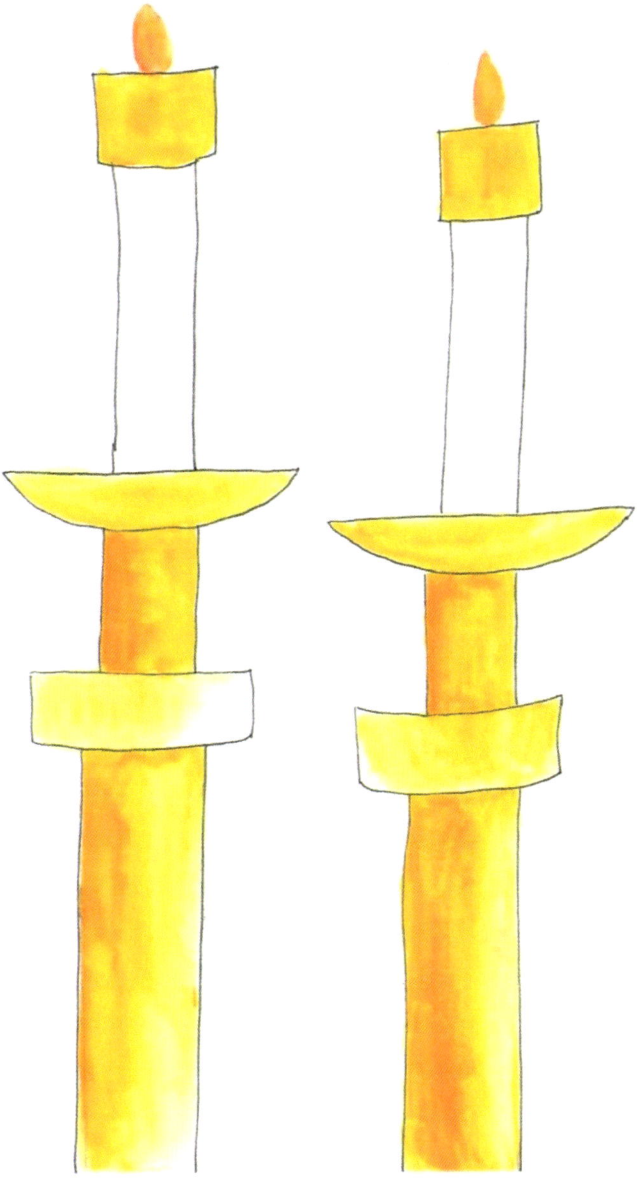

Chalice

Location: sanctuary (stored in sacristy)
Used during Mass: yes
Description:
This beautiful cup is used to hold the wine that becomes the Blood of Christ in the Eucharist. Because it holds the Precious Blood, it is made of a precious medal (gold or silver) and is often decorated with precious stones or similar ornamentation.

Chalice Veil

Location: sanctuary (stored in sacristy)
Used during Mass: yes
Description:
A special cloth that is used to cover the chalice on the altar when not in use (i.e. before the Eucharistic prayer). The fabric of this cloth may be beautifully decorated and be different colors in keeping with the liturgical season. It sometimes is made to match the vestments worn by the priest, using the same fabric.

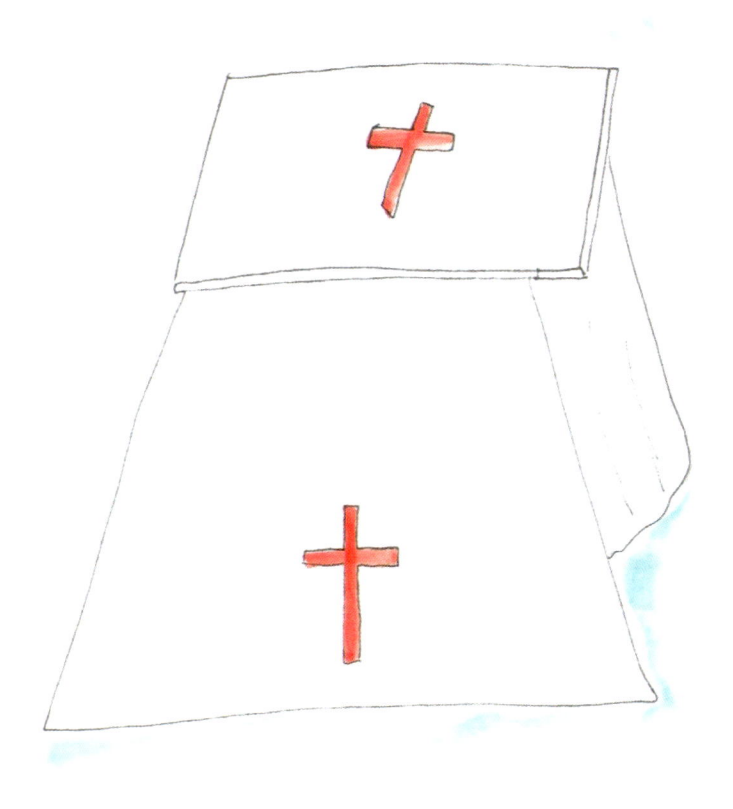

Ciborium

Location: sanctuary (stored in sacristy or tabernacle)
Used during Mass: yes
Description:
This is the sacred vessel used to hold the bread (hosts) that become the Body of Christ in the Eucharist. After Communion, if any of the Body of Christ remains, the ciborium is placed in the tabernacle.

Clacker

Location: sanctuary (stored in sacristy)
Used during Mass: yes
Description:
Typically, altar bells are used at the moment of consecration (when the bread and wine become the Body and Blood of Christ). However, for the Holy Thursday liturgy (and until the Easter Vigil) the clacker is used. It is a less joyous implement that can still be used to draw attention to what is happening on the altar.

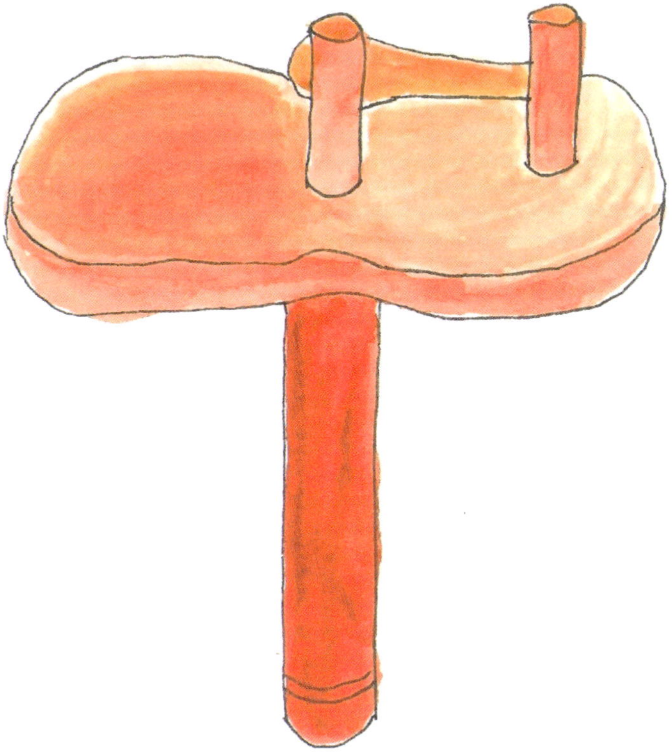

Corporal

Location: on the altar (extras stored in sacristy)
Used during Mass: yes
Description:
With its roots in the Latin word for "body," the corporal is a cloth that is unfolded and placed on the altar during the Eucharistic prayer. Were any of the particles of the Body of Christ or drops of the Blood of Christ to fall on the altar, the corporal would catch them. The corporal can be washed and rinsed in the sacrarium, a sink that drains directly into the ground (instead of the sewer) if needed. It is another special article that is used to show as much reverence to the Body and Blood of Christ as possible.

Crosier

Location: stored in cathedral sacristy
Used during Mass: yes
Description:
This is the staff used by the bishop or archbishop at Mass. It is meant to remind us of the crook of the Good Shepherd. The call of the bishop is to lovingly shepherd the people (the "sheep") of his diocese.

101

Crucifix

Location: sanctuary
Used during Mass: yes
Description:
This special cross, bearing the image of the crucified Christ, must be hung somewhere in the sanctuary or be on the altar. This depiction of Christ crucified calls to mind the representation (making present again) of the love and sacrifice of Christ on the cross at every Mass. The sacrifice on the cross is not repeated, but rather it is made real and present to all at Mass again, as if the faithful were at the foot of the cross.

I

Cruets

Location: credence (side) table in sanctuary (or at a credence table in the nave or vestibule, prior to the Offertory and the Presentation of the Gifts)

Used during Mass: yes

Description:
These two small containers hold the wine and water. Mingled together, they become the Blood of Christ at the consecration. At the Offertory, a small amount of water is mixed in with the wine. The mixing of the water and wine calls to mind Christ uniting human nature to his divine nature.

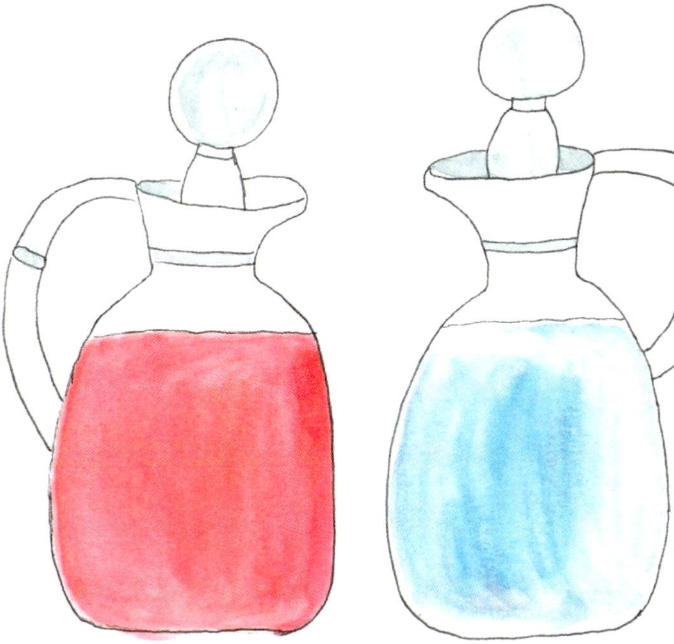

Funeral Pall

Location: put on casket in nave
Used during Mass: yes
Description:
Used for funerals, this white cloth covers the casket (which contains the body of the deceased person) during Mass. Its whiteness is reminiscent of the baptismal garment. The baptismal garment is worn at the beginning of a person's journey to heaven, and the pall recognizes the completion of the earthly portion of that journey, and the hope of heaven.

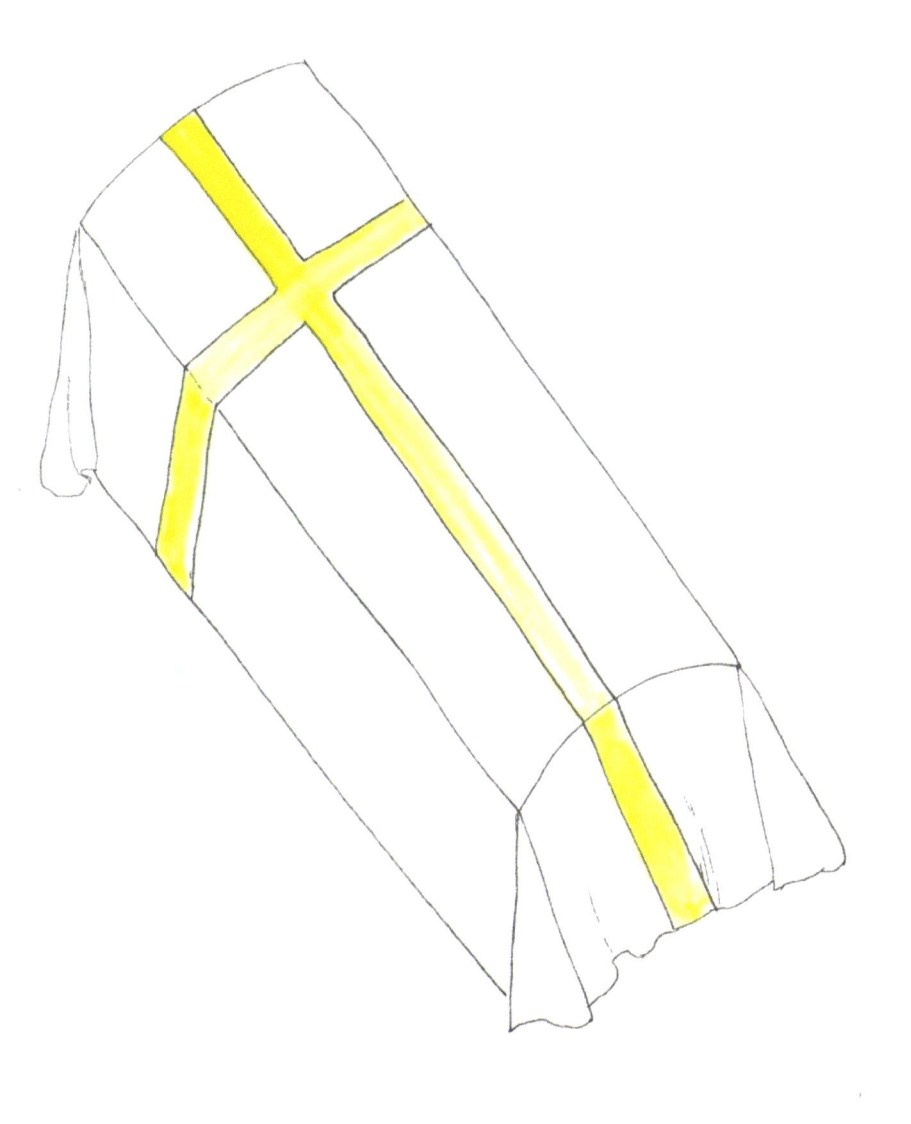

Holy Oils

Location: typically kept in a cabinet in the sanctuary (storage sometimes built into the wall or the sanctuary)

Used during Mass: sometimes

Description:

These oils are blessed or consecrated at the Chrism Mass. The Chrism Mass is typically celebrated by the bishop and the priests of the diocese on the morning of Holy Thursday, at the cathedral of the diocese. The Oil of the Sick and the Oil of Catechumens are blessed, meant to be used for the Anointing of the Sick (Oil of the Sick) and Baptism (Oil of Catechumens). The Sacred Chrism oil, however, is consecrated, i.e. set apart as something particularly holy. This fragrant oil is used at Baptisms, Confirmations, to consecrate a new altar, and to ordain a deacon, priest, or bishop.

Host

Location: in paten or ciborium on altar
Used during Mass: yes
Description:
This special, unleavened bread is made very simply – of only flour and water. In the Roman rite, this is the shape of the bread that becomes the Body of Christ through transubstantiation (the word for the transformation of the bread into the Body of Christ and the wine into the Blood of Christ) at Mass. After consecration, it still looks, tastes, and smells like bread, but it has become the Body of Christ, sacramentally present. The look, taste, and smell of the bread are called its "accidents," and they no longer belong to the bread, but to the Body of Christ.

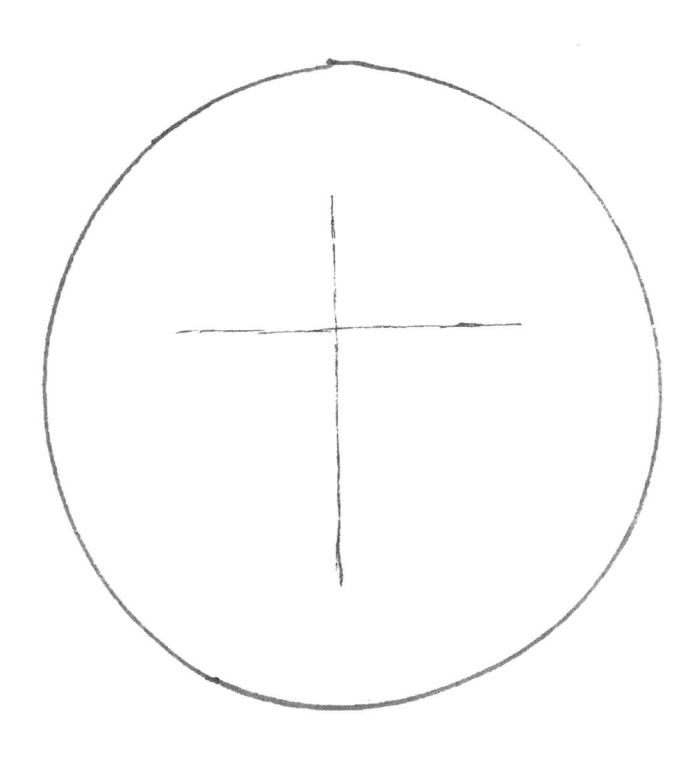

Lavabo

Location: kept in the sacristy
Used during Mass: yes
Description:
This beautiful bowl (made of glass or crystal) is used by the priest during the offertory. The priest pours water from the cruet over his hands (or does so with the assistance of an altar server), as he prays that he may be "cleansed" of his sin. The priest acknowledges his own unworthiness, and humbly turns to God for the grace to offer the sacrifice of the Mass (i.e., to make Christ's sacrifice on the cross present again, through the gift of the Eucharist). The priest offers the Mass *in persona Christi* – in the person of Christ, humbly putting himself totally under the service of Christ.

Organ

Location: nave or choir loft
Used during Mass: yes
Description:
This beautiful instrument is used to play music for Mass and other liturgies outside of Mass (such as public prayer of the Liturgy of the Hours). In the Roman rite, it is considered the traditional, preferable instrument for Mass (although other instruments may be used).

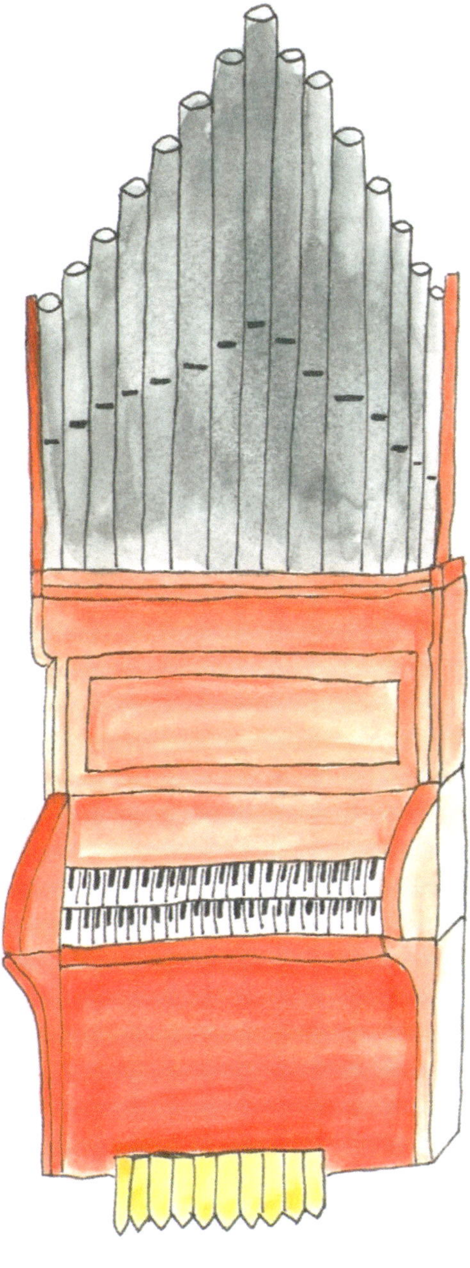

Paschal Candle

Location: sanctuary (during the Easter season and funerals) or beside the baptismal font (during the rest of the time)

Used during Mass: yes

Description:

This tall candle is used during Baptisms, funerals, and throughout the Easter season. A new one is blest at the Easter Vigil every year. In the blessing prayed by the priest, he recalls that all of time belongs to Christ. It is first lit from the Paschal fire and carried into the darkened church by the deacon at the beginning of the Easter Vigil. It is a symbol of Christ, who is our Light, and of his resurrection, which dispels the darkness of sin and death.

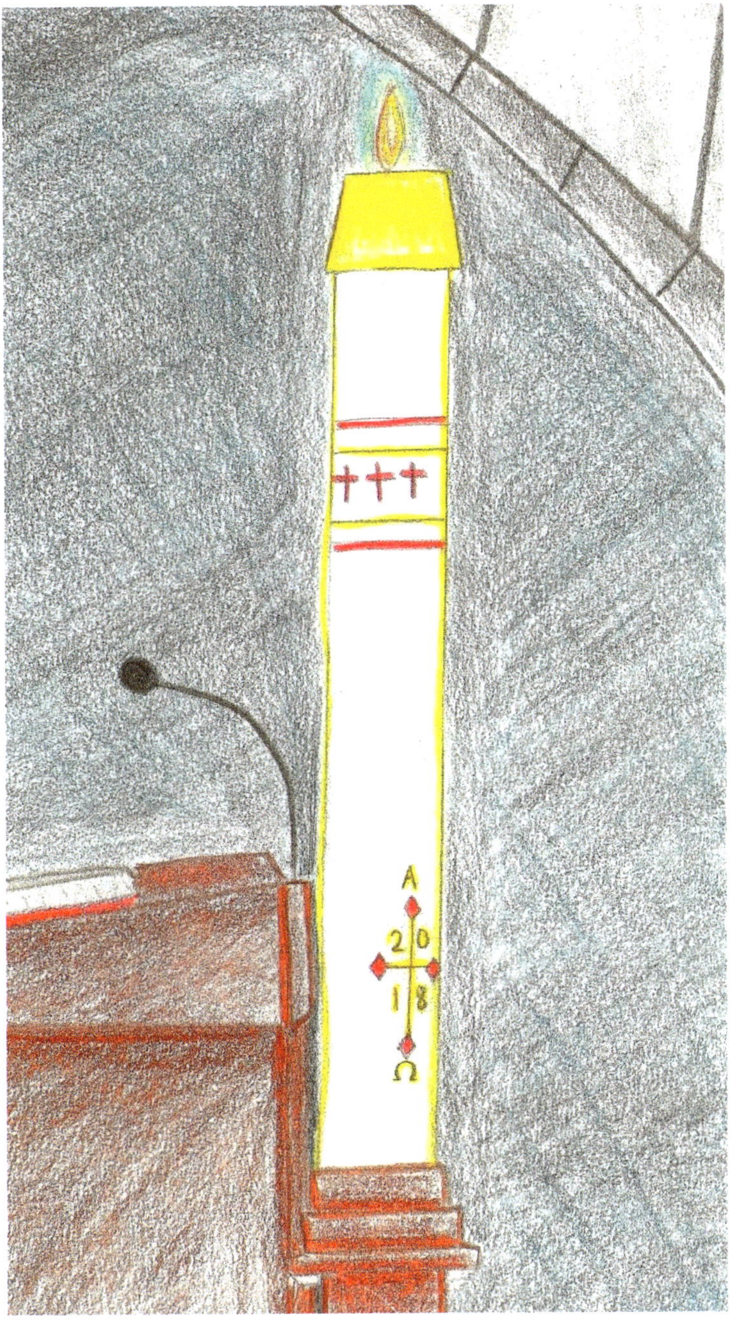
A
20
18
Ω

Paten

Location: on the altar (stored in sacristy)
Used during Mass: yes
Description:
This term refers to the flat, golden dish used to hold the presider's host at Mass (i.e., the large host that the priest elevates during the consecration). It also refers to the flat, golden dish, attached to a long handle, that is placed beneath the mouths of the faithful at Communion, to catch any fallen particles of the Body of Christ.

Pew
Location: nave
Used during Mass: yes
Description:
Although, historically, Catholic churches were built without any seating (the faithful would stand during the Mass) in more recent centuries, pews have often been used for seating during Mass.

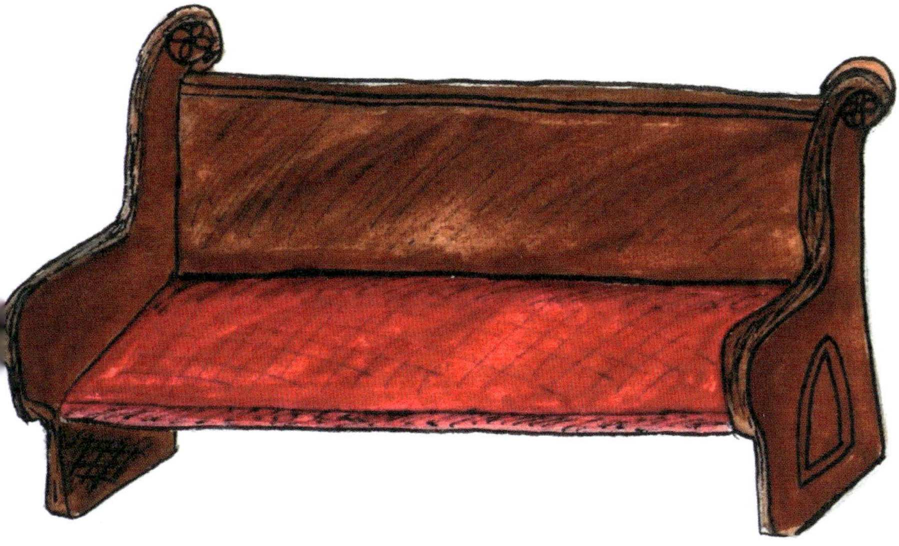

Presider's Chair

Location: sanctuary
Used during Mass: yes
Description:
This is the place where the priest sits during the Mass. It is a chair specifically for use by the priest (although may also be used by a presiding bishop). It is typically placed off to the side of the sanctuary, in a visible location, facing the altar.

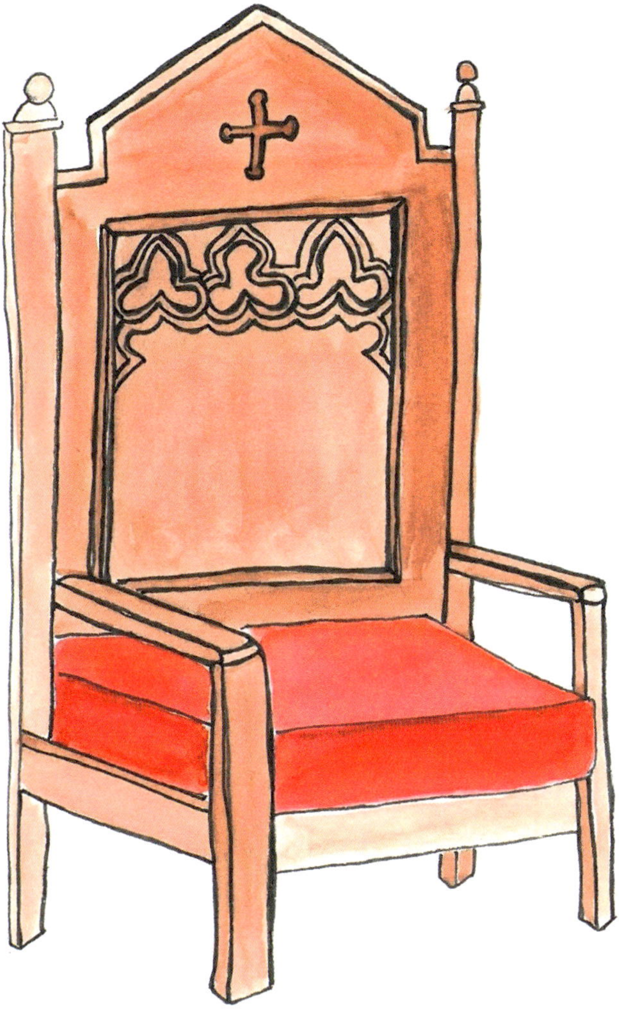

Processional Cross

Location: sanctuary (sometimes stored in sacristy)
Used during Mass: yes
Description:
This cross (typically a crucifix) is carried by an altar server during the opening and recessional (closing) processions at Mass. If candles are used in the procession, they are carried on each side of the processional cross. The processional cross leads the liturgical procession at Mass (unless incense is used, in which case, the incense leads the procession).

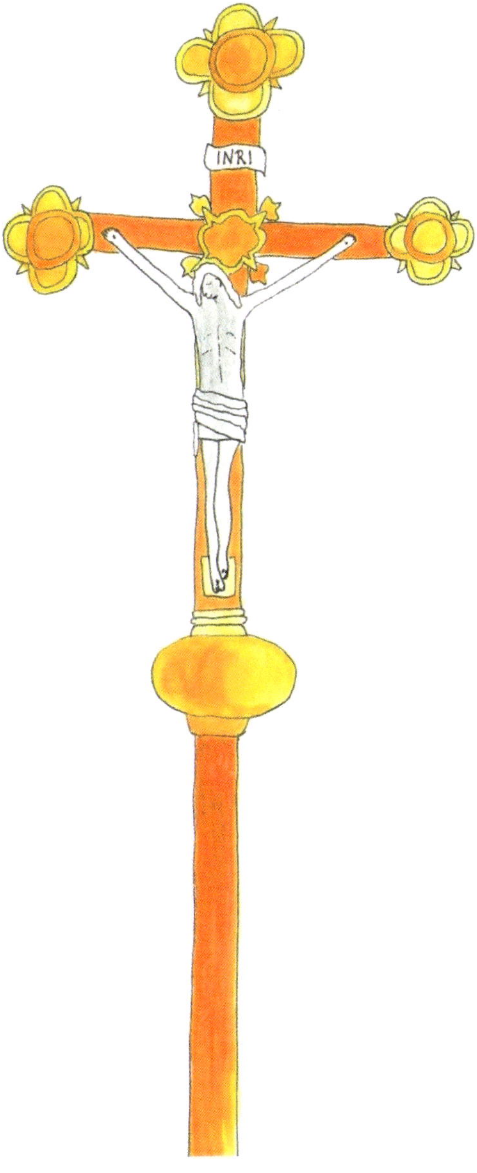
INRI

Purificator

Location: stored in sacristy (placed on the altar during Mass)
Used during Mass: yes
Description:
This cloth is used to wipe the chalice. It is used before consecration when the wine is poured into the chalice at the Offertory. It is used after the consecration, to wipe the chalice when the Blood of Christ is received by the priest or the faithful.

Pyx

Location: stored in sacristy (when not in use)
Used during Mass: yes
Description:
This golden container is small enough to be carried in a pocket, and it is closed and opened with a clasp. It is used to carry the Body of Christ, when the Eucharist is being brought to those who are sick or homebound by a priest, deacon, or extraordinary minister (i.e. a lay person assisting in distribution of the Eucharist).

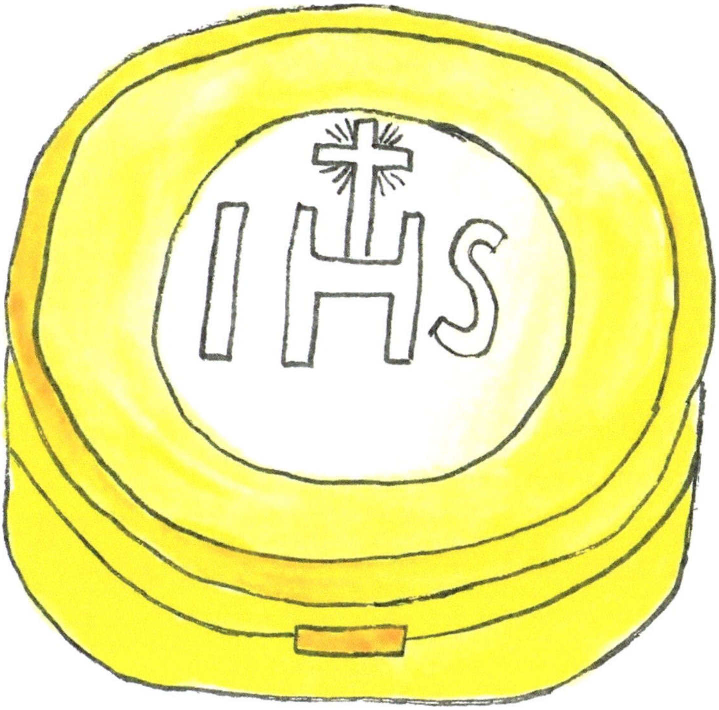
IHS

Sanctuary Lamp

Location: sanctuary

Used during Mass: yes (although remains lit outside of Mass, too)

Description:

A beeswax candle in a red, glass holder, this light is found near the tabernacle. When it is lit, it is a sign that the Body of Christ is present in the tabernacle. It is a sign of God's presence in the church. The sanctuary lamp is extinguished after Jesus is removed from the altar of repose on Holy Thursday and is relit when Jesus is again placed in the tabernacle at the Easter Vigil. This absence is a reminder of the time that Jesus suffered and died on the cross and was buried in the tomb.

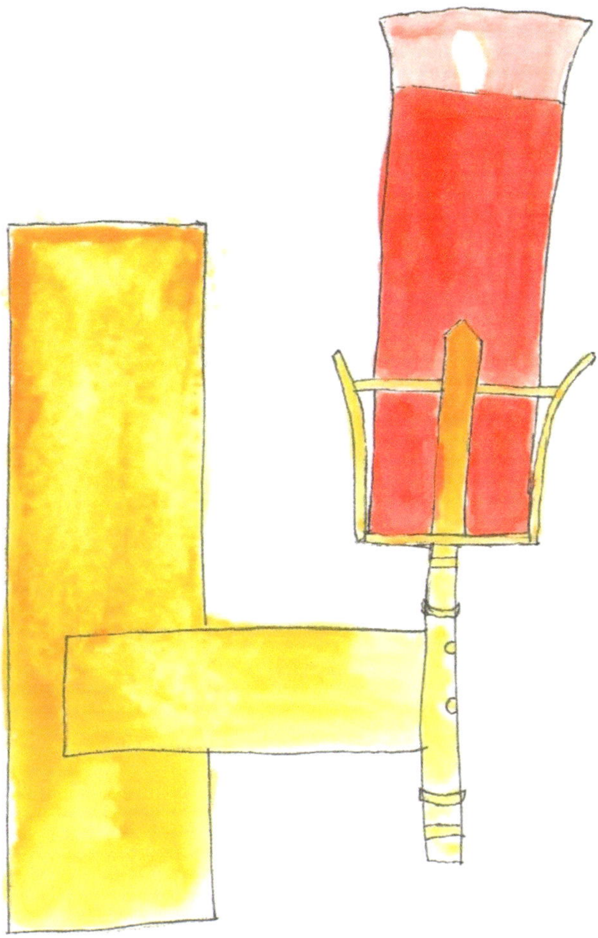

Stained Glass Window

Location: nave, sanctuary, vestibule, and sacristy

Used during Mass: visible during Mass

Description:

These beautiful windows are found in almost every Catholic church, chapel, or cathedral. They typically depict scenes from the Scriptures, lives of the saints, or the history of the diocese. Like icons, statues, and other religious art, they are meant to raise the minds and hearts of the faithful to God and to teach about the faith.

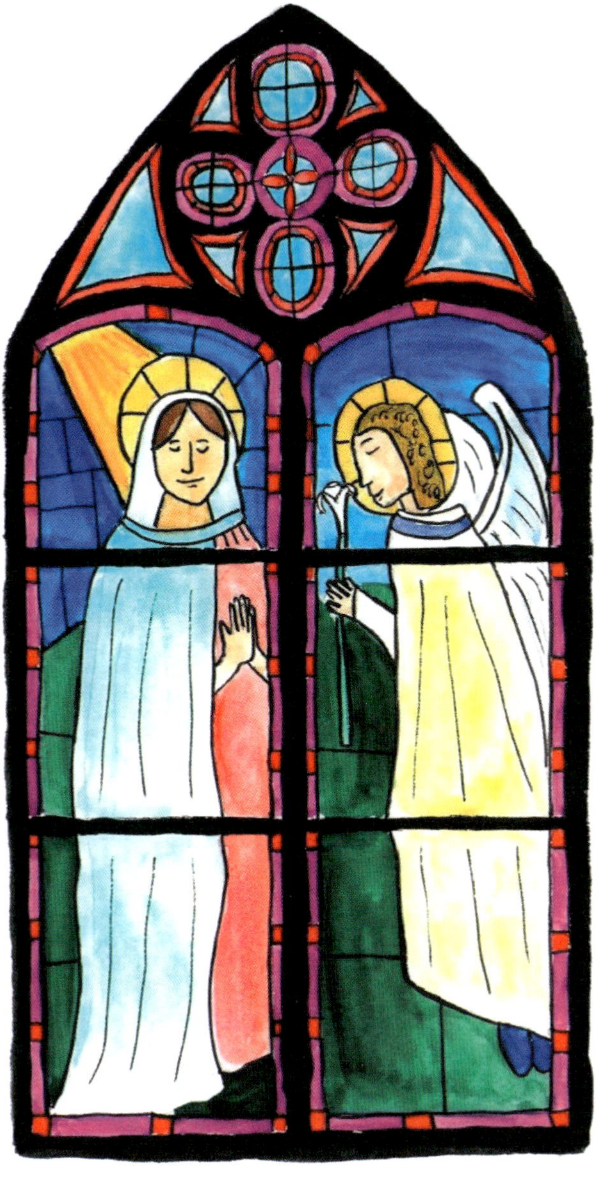

Statue

Location: nave or sanctuary
Used during Mass: no
Description:
Statues are another form of religious art, meant to help raise minds and hearts to God in prayer. Catholics do not worship statues, since worship is for God alone. Catholics venerate statues—that is, treat them with special care, since they serve as reminders of Jesus and of the saints, men and women who have gone to heaven before us. Kneeling before or kissing a statue is a sign of veneration, not worship; it is a sign of love for God and the saints, like the tenderness with which images and belongings of loved ones who are deceased are regarded.

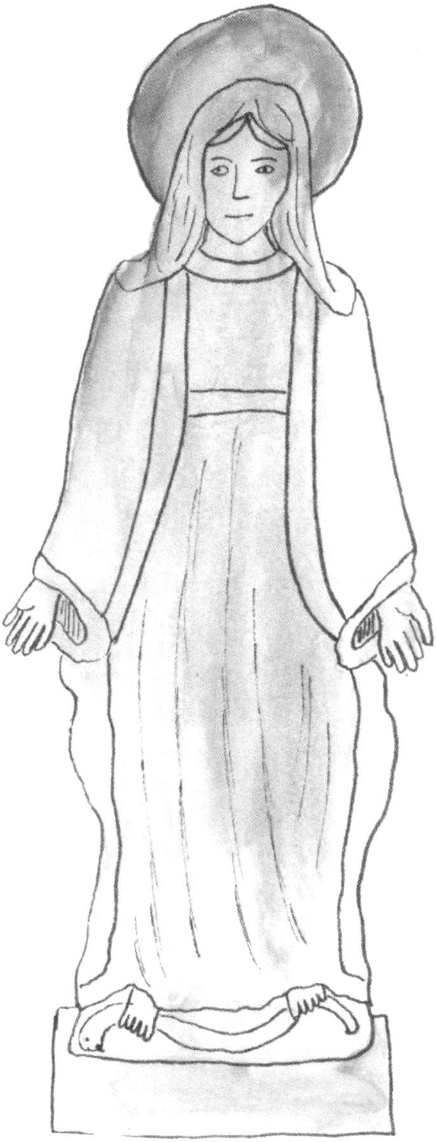

Tabernacle

Location: sanctuary
Used during Mass: yes
Description:
This beautiful golden container, typically box-like in shape, is used to house the Eucharist, the Body of Christ, after Mass. (It also can be locked with a small key, to prevent the Eucharist from being stolen from the church.) The Eucharist is said to be "reserved in the tabernacle," meaning that Christ is ever present and ever available for those who are sick or ailing and in need of Communion. The faithful may visit the church outside of Mass, to pray to Jesus, and spend time in his Eucharistic presence. The word "tabernacle" originates from the Old Testament, when God first promised to be present among his people, in a sacred place that was set apart.

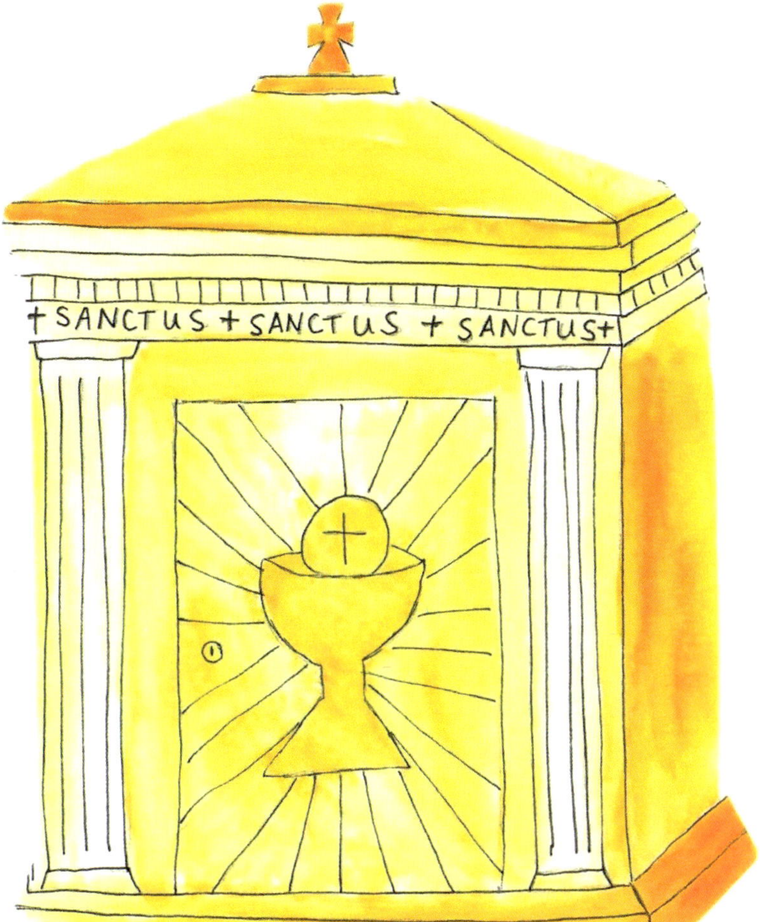
+ SANCTUS + SANCTUS + SANCTUS +

Thurible (censor) and incense boat

Location: sanctuary (stored in sacristy)
Used during Mass: yes
Description:
Containing a lit piece of charcoal with fragments of incense sprinkled on top, the smoke of the incense fills the church when the thurible is swung on its chain. (Additional incense is kept in the boat.) The incense smoke is a sign of our prayers rising to God, fragrant and pleasing in his sight. Incense is typically used in the opening procession and closing recessional, before the Gospel, during the Offertory, and during the Eucharistic prayer. The priest or deacon will bow before and after incensing the faithful. The faithful bow in return.

Wine

Location: sanctuary
Used during Mass: yes
Description:
A drink made from grapes and containing some amount of alcohol, wine is the matter consecrated into the Blood of Christ. As with the host, after becoming the Blood of Christ, the "accidents" (i.e. taste, smell, sight) of the wine remain the same, but it is no longer wine, but the substance of the Blood of Christ (and those "accidents" now belong to the Blood of Christ, not the wine). Like the bread, wine is used because it is the substance Christ used at the Last Supper, when he gave the gift of the Eucharist to his Church.

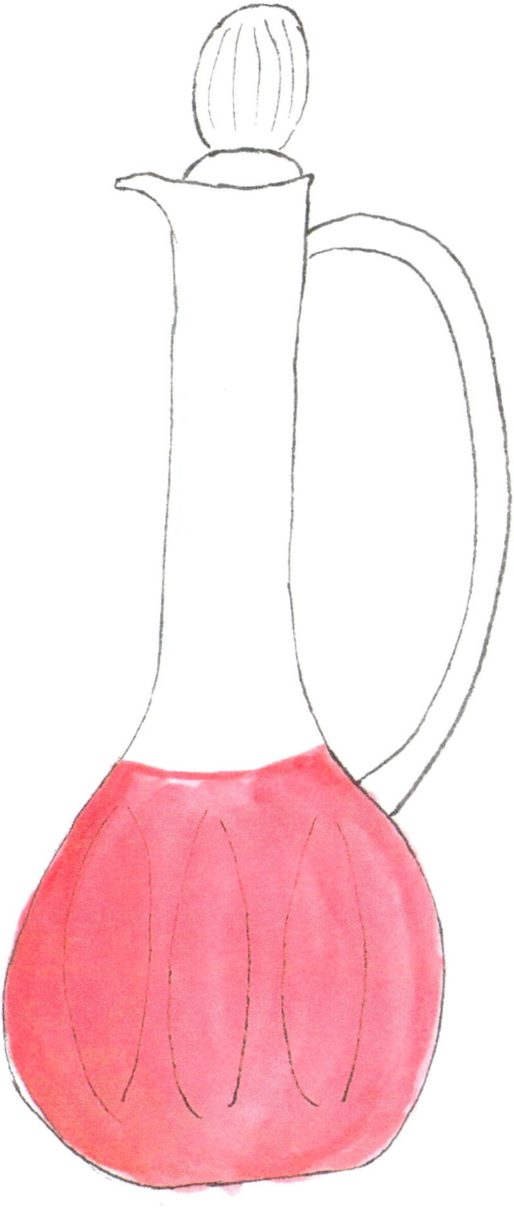

Books

The Mass is a liturgy – a prayer that is structured, rather than spontaneous. The books used during the Mass contain prayers, hymns, and readings from Scripture. The same prayers are prayed, and the same Scriptures are read at Masses throughout the world.

Book of the Gospels

Location: sanctuary (stored in sacristy)
Used during Mass: yes
Description:
This beautiful book contains the Gospel readings found in the Lectionary. It is often carried into the church during the opening procession and is then placed on the altar. When it is time for the Gospel to be read, the priest or deacon will process with it to the ambo during the Alleluia and may incense it as a sign of reverence for God's Word. The symbols on the cover represent each of the Gospel writers: Matthew (a man), Mark (a lion with wings), Luke (an ox with wings), and John (an eagle).

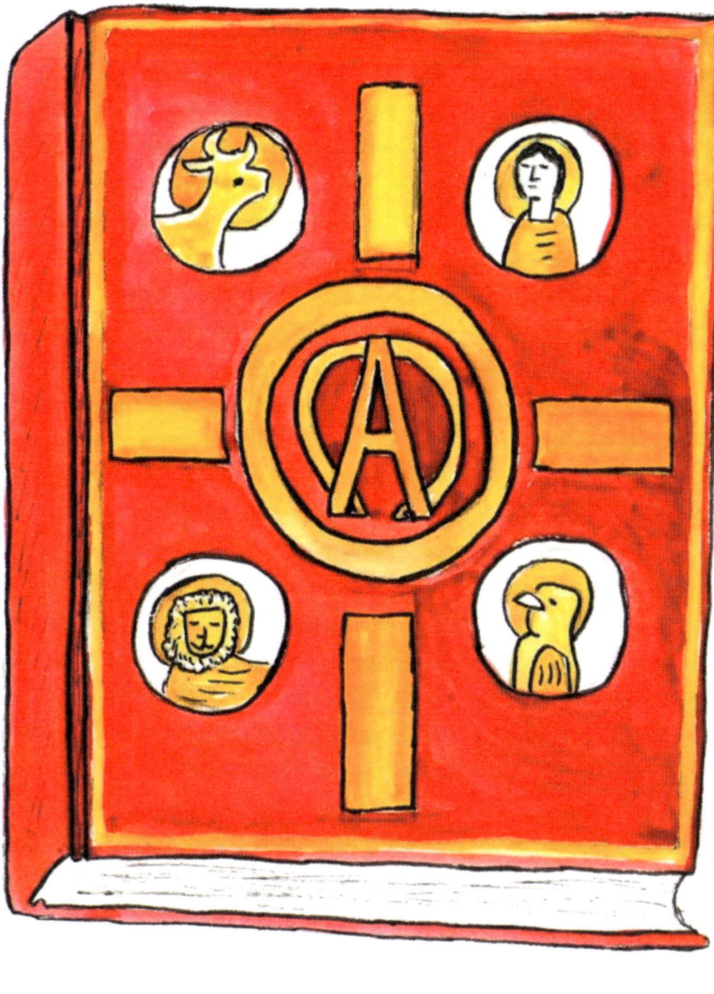

Hymnal

Location: nave (in the pews)
Used during Mass: yes
Description:
This book contains the hymns, antiphons, and psalms sung at Mass. Many also contain additional material, such as Mass responses and Mass parts.

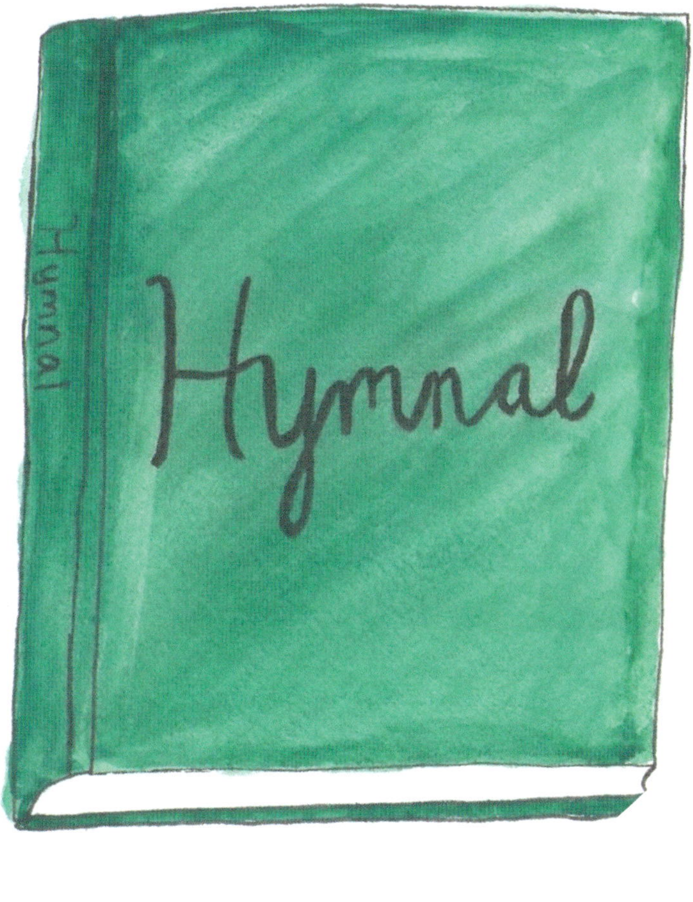
Hymnal
Hymnal

Lectionary

Location: sanctuary (stored in sacristy)
Used during Mass: yes
Description:
This book contains all the Scripture readings for the Mass. It contains the readings for all the Sunday cycles of readings (Year A, B, and C) and the readings for the weekday reading cycles (Year I and II). The lector reads the first and second readings and responsorial psalm from this book, and the deacon or priest may read the Gospel from it, if not using the Book of the Gospels. During the Mass, it sits on the ambo.

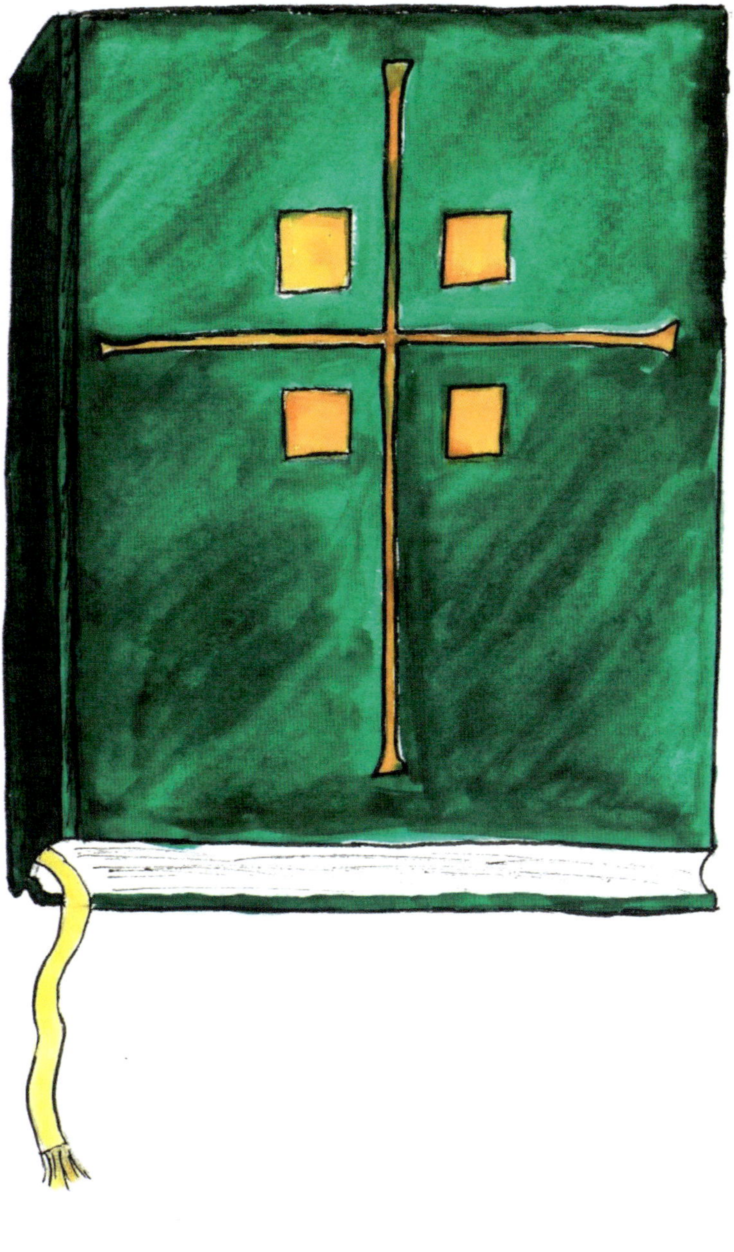

Roman Missal

Location: sanctuary/on the altar (stored in sacristy)
Used during Mass: yes
Description:
This book contains all the prayers used during Mass, including the Opening and Closing Prayers, the Eucharistic Prayer, etc. It also contains the rubrics for the liturgy (i.e. the instructions for the priest that describe how to celebrate the Mass, as well as how to celebrate special Masses and liturgies, like the Triduum liturgies). The prayers are written in black lettering, and the rubrics in red.

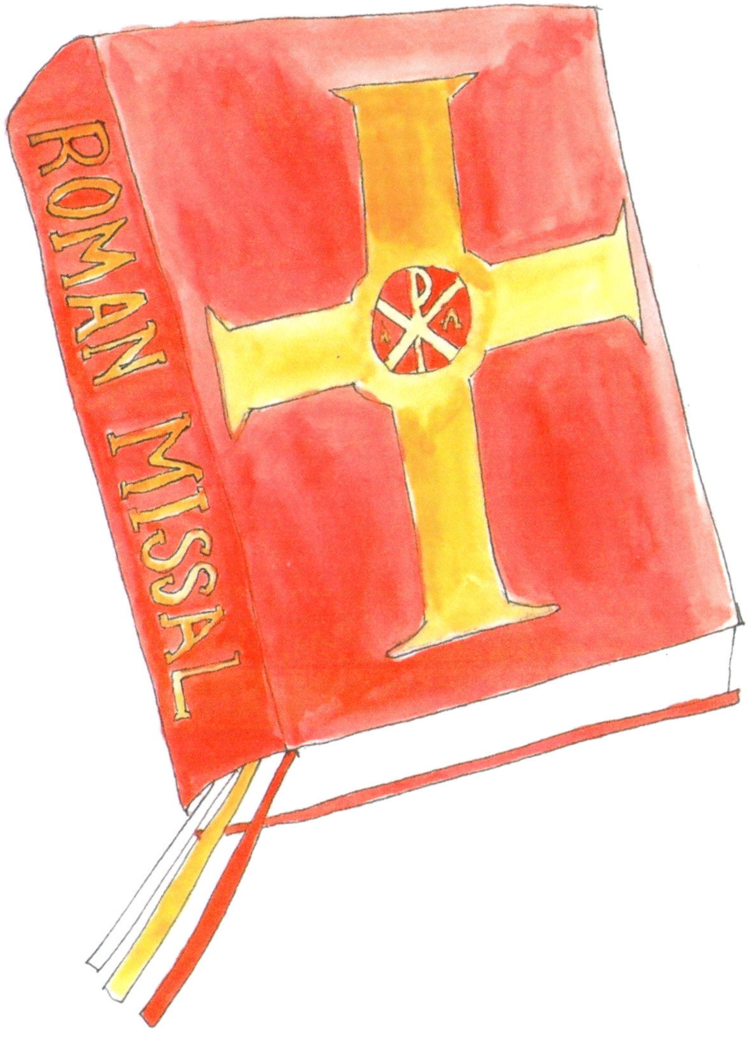
ROMAN MISSAL

Index (alphabetical)

Ablution Cup 76
Alb 10
Altar 54
Altar Bells 78
Altar Cloth 80
Ambo 56
Amice 12
Aspergillium 82

Baldacchino 58
Baptismal Font 60
Baptismal Shell 84
Biretta 14
Book of the Gospels 144

Candle Snuffer 86
Candles 88
Cassock 16
Chalice 90
Chalice Veil 92
Chasuble 18
Ciborium 94
Cincture 20
Clacker 96
Confessional 62
Cope 22
Corporal 98
Crosier 100
Crucifix 102
Cruets 104

Dalmatic 24

Funeral Pall 106

Holy Oils 108
Holy Water Font 36
Host 110
Hymnal 146

Icon 38
Kneeler 40

Lavabo 112
Lectionary 148

Miter 26
Monstrance 42

Nave 64

Organ 114

Paschal Candle 116
Paten 118
Pew 120
Presider's Chair 122
Processional Canopy 44
Processional Cross 124
Purificator 126
Pyx 128

Reliquary 46
Roman Missal 150

Sacrarium 66
Sacristy 68
Sanctuary 70
Sanctuary Lamp 130
Stained Glass Window 132
Stations of the Cross 48
Statue 134
Stole 28
Surplice 30

Tabernacle 136
Thurible 138

Vestibule 72
Votive Candles 50

Wine 140

Zucchetto 32

Sources:

The following links were helpful in researching the origin and use of the objects and vessels discussed in this book. The iBreviary app was also consulted to check wording in various rites and liturgies:

"Liturgy - The Baldacchino."
http://marques.silvaclan.net/?p=1191

https://www.catholiccompany.com/baptismal-shell-i115783/

http://catholicexchange.com/the-symbols-of-the-gospel-writers

https://en.wikipedia.org/wiki/Cincture

https://forums.catholic.com/showthread.php?t=179868

http://www.newadvent.org/cathen/10404a.htm

https://www.ewtn.com/expert/answers/music_and_instruments.htm

https://www.ewtn.com/library/Liturgy/zlitur84.htm

http://www.usccb.org/prayer-and-worship/the-mass/roman-missal/index.cfm

"Stole." http://www.newadvent.org/cathen/14301a.htm

Made in the USA
Columbia, SC
21 May 2018